Militarists
Merchants
and
Missionaries

United States Expansion in Middle America

Edited by
Eugene R. Huck & Edward H. Moseley

Essays Written in Honor of
Alfred Barnaby Thomas

University of Alabama Press
University, Alabama

Respectfully dedicated to our teacher and friend
Alfred Barnaby Thomas

Militarists
Merchants
and
Missionaries

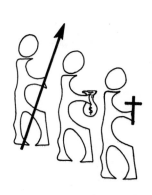

Alfred Barnaby Thomas

Contents

Contributors

Conwell A. Anderson *is President of Averett College, Danville, Virginia.*

John Francis Bannon, S.J. *is Professor of History at Saint Louis University, St. Louis, Missouri.*

Annadrue Brownback *is a teacher at Wakefield High School, Arlington, Virginia.*

Harold Edward Greer, Jr. *is Assistant Professor of History at Virginia Commonwealth University, Richmond, Virginia.*

Eugene R. Huck *is Chairman of the Division of Social Sciences at West Georgia College, Carrollton, Georgia.*

Herman Hupperich *is Assistant Professor of History at Southeastern Louisiana College, Hammond, Louisiana.*

Wilford H. Lane *is Assistant Professor of History at Virginia Polytechnic Institute, Blacksburg, Virginia.*

Edward H. Moseley *is Associate Professor of History at the University of Alabama, Tuscaloosa, Alabama.*

Wesley Phillips Newton *is Associate Professor of History at Auburn University, Auburn, Alabama.*

Fred Lamar Pearson, Jr. *is Associate Professor of History at Valdosta State College, Valdosta, Georgia.*

Wilkins B. Winn *is Associate Professor of History at East Carolina University, Greenville, North Carolina.*

Alfred Barnaby Thomas

Teachers come and teachers go, of course, but the influence of the better ones continues long after they have retired from the classroom; they live on in the memories of their students and in the work they do. It is not quite enough for students simply to say "thank you" for the guidance and friendship extended to them by an inspiring teacher. A more appropriate expression of gratitude might be a collection of essays that reflect the beneficial influence of the distinguished professor. It is just such a collection that is offered here as a *Festschrift* in tribute to Professor Alfred Barnaby Thomas.

Alfred Barnaby Thomas was born April 14, 1896 in Belt, Montana. After completing high school he moved south to Berkeley as an undergraduate at the University of California. The young Montanan soon fell under the spell of one of that institution's great teachers, Herbert Eugene Bolton. Bolton developed a new perspective on American history that emphasized the complex forces outside of the narrow English tradition and focused on the contributions of the French and Spanish in the colonization of the continent. Having uncovered more materials relating to the Spanish Borderlands than he could ever hope to research personally, Bolton welcomed the young undergraduate in whom he saw such fine potentialities. Thomas received a teaching fellowship when he entered graduate school and worked with Bolton on his famous course in the history of the Americas. Bolton assigned him the topic of the Spaniards in Colorado, and in 1924 Thomas earned his Master's degree with a thesis on that subject. In the latter part of 1924, he published two articles based on the same research, one an account of the Villasur expedition that ended disastrously at the forks of the Platte River, the other dealing with the activities of the Spanish in Colorado.* Bolton, meanwhile, encouraged him to become a candidate for the Ph.D. degree and assigned him the vast territory to the north and east of Santa Fe as *his* area of research.

In 1925–26 the Department of History offered the young scholar a rare opportunity to continue his studies. Some years earlier, the Native Sons of the Golden West, a California organization, had established an endowment to provide annual grants for research in foreign countries to two of the most promising graduate students in the department. The N.S.G.W. fellows were to be distinguished

* For a complete list of the publications of Dr. Thomas, see Appendix.

men or, better, young men destined to become truly distinguished historians. In recommending Alfred Thomas for the honor, Bolton wrote:

> Mr. Thomas is a man of unusual qualities. He is a graduate of the University of California and also took his Master's degree here in Western history. For the past two years he has been a teaching fellow with me in the same course. He is studying problems connected with the opening of overland routes by Spain to California and the Pacific Coast. He will gather materials in Spain for further work on that topic....

The History Committee of the Native Sons acted favorably on the recommendation, and in the fall of 1925 Thomas traveled to Spain for an exciting and profitable year of research at the Archivo General de Indias and other depositories. Upon his return to California in mid-1926, Thomas was granted a resident fellowship, and spent the following academic year at Berkeley writing his dissertation and preparing for his examinations. He finished his dissertation, "Spanish Expeditions Northeast of New Mexico," took his final oral examination in late summer, and accepted a teaching position at the University of Oklahoma. He remained at that institution for the next ten years, except during 1929–30 when he returned to Spain on a Guggenheim Fellowship.

Research completed during those ten years at Norman, despite heavy teaching loads, more than fulfilled the promise that Bolton had seen in his young scholar. In 1932 Thomas published his *Forgotten Frontiers: A Study of the Spanish-Indian Policy of Juan Bautista de Anza, Governor of New Mexico, 1777–1787*, a work that remains "of the first importance to all those who would understand Spanish imperialism in North America," as Maurice Halperin characterized it in a review in *The New Republic*. Three years later, in 1935, Thomas published a second major study, *After Coronado: Spanish Explorations Northeast of New Mexico, 1696–1727*, which Oliver La Farge commended in *The Saturday Review of Literature* as "an important addition to our history, and a rounded picture of a forgotten empire. . . ." During those Oklahoma years Thomas also published a dozen articles in a number of learned journals. By the end of the decade, he was an acknowledged authority not only in his specialty, the Borderlands, but also in the whole field of Latin American history.

In the spring of 1937, when the University of Alabama decided to develop a program in Latin American history, Herbert Bolton commended Thomas to the attention of Dr. A. B. Moore, Dean of the Graduate School, characterizing Thomas as "an unusually good man . . . enthusiastic for his work, and a fine teacher." Professor Thomas went to Tuscaloosa in the fall of 1937 to begin a new phase of his career. At the University of Alabama, he devoted thirty years to research, teaching, and the direction of graduate work.

In 1940 his third major book appeared, *The Plains Indians and New Mexico, 1751–1778*. The following year he published *Teodoro de Croix and the Northern Frontier of New Spain, 1776–1783*. During the years at Alabama, Thomas also turned his attention toward the eastern Borderlands, giving added emphasis to the role of the Spanish in that region. On one occasion Bolton commented regarding this work: "You have put the history of the Gulf region and the lower Mississippi Valley 'in a new mold,' as Turner once said of one of my contributions."

From the latter 1940's through the 1950's Thomas focused his attention on the broader field of Latin America. Circumstances and availability of materials for his students did much to turn him into a Latin Americanist. He became a regular commentator on aspects of the contemporary Latin American scene. Two dozen or more of his articles appeared in various numbers of *The Delphian Quarterly*. In 1956 Macmillan brought out his college survey, *Latin America: A History*.

In the late 1950's a new kind of project brought the professor back to an earlier interest, the Indians of the Southwest. The Indian Claims Commission was adjudicating a series of cases involving the first Americans and turned to Thomas to furnish them with information on the Jicarilla Apache, the Mescalero-Chiricahua Apache, the Lipan Apache, and the Yavapai. These were old friends revisited, inasmuch as Thomas had previously uncovered extensive materials dealing with these Indians during his early researches.

Alfred Thomas led a full and fruitful life as a scholar and a teacher. During his years at the University of Alabama, he left his professional stamp on thousands of undergraduates and directed the work of over sixty graduate students, many of whom, inspired by his example, went into the teaching profession. They will keep alive the Borderlands tradition and interpret America's Iberian heritage with sympathy and understanding.

JOHN FRANCIS BANNON, S.J.

Militarists
Merchants
and
Missionaries

Introduction

Eugene R. Huck and
Edward H. Moseley

Spain led the way for the European colonization of the New World. From the Caribbean base established in the late fifteenth century, the Spanish explorers and colonizers pushed westward to Mexico, southward to Panama and South America, and northward into the region they called Florida. By 1598, the Hapsburg colonial empire in America stretched from Chile to Chesapeake Bay. Not until 1607 did the English succeed in establishing their first foothold in the Americas at Jamestown, a small settlement on the northern fringe of the Spanish empire.

This humble English settlement on the Atlantic coast of North America, however, was a beginning point of a nation that was to become a dominant world power three centuries later. This development involved the expansion of Anglo-American settlers westward and southward into territory that had been explored, claimed, and partly colonized by Spain. Not only did the British push into the Florida territory, but they also struck at the very heart of the Spanish system, the Caribbean region. This English penetration took on the character of a commercial as well as a territorial struggle, since it also involved a contest for Indian alliances and markets.

Anglo-American expansion continued throughout the colonial period, and the new nation that won its independence in 1783 continued the process. Many United States political leaders stressed what they considered the need for expansion, and found a justification for it in the doctrine of Manifest Destiny. With the Louisiana Purchase, the Adams-Onis Treaty, and the victory of the United States in the Mexican War, the nation became a two-ocean power. As a result of these events and expanding economic interests, Anglo-American influence was greatly increased in the Gulf of Mexico and the Caribbean Sea. Consequently, the region of Middle America came to be of special interest to the United States.

Following the Treaty of Guadalupe Hidalgo, the expansion southward into the Gulf and Caribbean area took on a new character and concentrated on new objectives. Increasing investments, the Spanish-American War, and the acquisition of the Canal Zone were major aspects of this process. The phenomenal growth of the political and economic influence of the United States is well known. There is often a tendency, however, for observers to overlook the extent of Anglo-American penetration into Middle America. The essays in this collection treat various aspects of this ever-increasing influence. They point clearly to the interrelationship between diplomatic and military conflicts with political schemes, commercial enterprises, and missionary zeal. It is hoped that by focusing on such diverse aspects of the expansion process these studies will give a new insight into that movement and will illuminate its unity and complexity. Perhaps they will even provide a clearer perspective for viewing the complex relationship which exists today between the United States and the nations of Latin America.

There is a major factor that unifies the essays in this volume. Each of the contributors was privileged to receive his historical training and guidance under the direction of Dr. Alfred B. Thomas, Professor Emeritus of History at the University of Alabama. It was under his influence and inspiration that each of the contributors undertook a career in Latin American history. Hence it is to Dr. Thomas that this volume is dedicated.

Many individuals contributed to the preparation of this *Festschrift*. Dr. Charles G. Summersell, Head of the Department of History at the University of Alabama, gave invaluable assistance during the planning stages of the project. Members of the staff of the University of Alabama library have offered constant assistance, and George Jerry Morgan has helped to trace down a number of elusive citations. Miss Sara Mayfield has given unstintingly of her time and talents to guide the editors, and has been an inspiration in bringing the volume to a conclusion.

The assistance of the Office for International Programs of the University of Alabama in supporting publication of this volume is gratefully acknowledged.

Anglo-Spanish Rivalry in the Georgia Country; 1670-1691

Fred Lamar Pearson, Jr.

The Spanish entered the Western Hemisphere in 1492, and by 1512 they had successfully established colonies on the islands of Cuba, Hispaniola, and Puerto Rico. Plantations established on these islands produced sufficient quantities of grain and herds of cattle to furnish supplies for further Spanish expansion in the New World. Soon after establishing these supply bases in the Caribbean, Spanish *conquistadores* discovered the Florida peninsula and entered the interior searching for the "Jordan River," the "Fountain of Youth," and mineral wealth. Juan Ponce de León, Lucas Vásquez de Ayllón, Pánfilo de Narváez, Hernando de Soto, Fray Luis de Cáncer, and Tristán de Luna y Arellano headed six major expeditions to Florida.

Ayllón established his settlement, San Miguel de Gualdape, near present-day Georgetown, South Carolina, in 1526. The combination of disease, inclement weather, and a shortage of supplies thinned the colonists' ranks. Ayllón's untimely death soon after the establishment of San Miguel prompted the remaining settlers to retire to Santo Domingo,[1] and Spain sent no further colonizing expeditions to Florida until 1558. Meanwhile, the Bahama Channel, the return route to Europe for the Spanish treasure galleons, became increasingly more attractive to pirates. Caribbean hurricanes moved frequently through the channel and wrecked many galleons on the Florida littoral, where Indian inhabitants murdered the crews. Spanish authorities, impressed with the need for an outpost on Florida's east coast, dispatched Tristán de Luna y Arellano in 1558 to establish a colony at Santa Elena (present-day Port Royal, South Carolina). Luna, who had been second-in-command on Francisco Vásquez de Coronado's expedition, landed first at Pensacola. A hurricane struck his force and destroyed or severely damaged most of the ships and supplies. After dispatching messengers to Mexico for relief, Luna traveled with most of the colonists into Alabama in search of food, leaving a token force at Pensacola. Luna returned to Pensacola after a year's absence and was relieved of his command by Angel de Villafañe. The new commander led the colonists on to the Carolinas in search of a suitable site on which to establish a colony. Failing to find such a site, Villafañe returned with the remnants of the Luna expedition to Santo Domingo.[2]

The expedition had hardly returned to Hispaniola when Jean Ribaut led a group of French Huguenots to Port Royal, South Carolina. Ribaut's colonizing effort failed, but René de Laudonnière succeeded in establishing a colony of Huguenots at Fort Caroline near the mouth of the St. Johns River in 1564.[3] News of these French intrusions alarmed the Spaniards; the presence of the fort, especially, threatened Spain's control of the Bahama Channel. King Philip II selected Pedro Menéndez de Avilés to remove the French menace and to establish a colony in Florida. Menéndez led more than a thousand colonists to Florida in 1565 and spent more than a million dollars of his personal fortune in establishing a permanent settlement at St. Augustine. Soon after landing at St. Augustine, Menéndez moved against the French. In 1565, he captured Fort Caroline, executed all the French except Catholics, and renamed the seized bastion Fort San Mateos. The French threat having been removed, Menéndez set out to fortify Florida.[4]

At Santa Elena the new commander constructed Fort San Felipe, established friendly relations with the Guale Indians[5] along the Georgia seacoast and on the offshore islands, and posted a garrison on Santa Catalina Island (presently, St. Catherines). Not neglectful of the interior regions, Governor Menéndez dispatched Captain Juan Pardo and Sergeant Hernando Boyano in 1566 to develop a road from Santa Elena to Zacatecas, Mexico. He hoped that Spanish treasure could be moved overland, thus avoiding the dangers of pirates and bad weather in the Bahama Channel. Pardo made two trips into the interior and traveled as far west as Alabama. He established defensive outposts, but insufficient support and Indian hostility forced the Spanish to abandon them.[6] The road that Menéndez hoped to develop was never built. Meanwhile, however, the commander endeavoured to colonize Florida and to fortify the area; he also sought to introduce Catholicism to the aboriginal inhabitants of the Southeast.

Jesuit missionaries arrived in Florida in 1566, but misfortune befell them. The vessel that brought the first group of missionaries landed not at St. Augustine but near the mouth of the St. Johns. A boat crew rowed Father Pedro Martínez, the superior, ashore to inquire of the Indians the direction to St. Augustine. While he was seeking Indians along the coast, a tempest arose and blew Father Martínez' vessel out to sea. Soon afterwards a band of hostile Indians attacked the party and killed the superior and most of his followers. In spite of this unfortunate beginning, the Jesuit effort soon showed promise. Father Domingo Agustín distinguished himself by writing a grammar in the Yamasee dialect and by preparing for the inhabitants of Guale a catechism in the same tongue. Father Bautista de Segura, who came to Florida in 1568, led a band of followers northward to Virginia in a determined effort to establish a permanent mission. In February, 1571 the Indians massacred all but one of Segura's followers. This disaster no doubt influenced greatly the decision of Jesuit authorities to pull out of Florida in the following year.[7]

The Franciscans moved into Florida in 1573 to replace the Jesuits. They worked long and hard to create an effective mission system, and they soon moved out from their headquarters at St. Augustine to establish missions and *doctrinas* in an evangelizing effort that covered a large section of the southeastern United States.[8] Among the most distinguished of these early Franciscan missionaries were Father Baltasar López and Father Alonso Reynoso.

For more than two decades the mission system flourished in Guale and the environs of St. Augustine. A revolt which broke out in Guale in 1597, however, threatened to undo all the missionary efforts. Juan, heir to the *mico*[9] of Tolomato,[10] led the uprising, and several of the missionaries suffered martyrdom as the rebellion swept through the missions. Governor Gonzalo Méndez Canzo (1596–1603) moved swiftly to put down the insurrection and to restore order to the mission fields. He dispatched soldiers to punish the rebellious Indians and to protect the remaining missionaries. Although the governor's punitive expedition failed to capture the Guale insurgents, the Spanish infantrymen burned several villages to the ground and destroyed valuable food supplies. This punishment convinced the Guale natives of the wisdom of reaffirming loyalty to the Spanish authorities, and the brown-robed Franciscans returned shortly afterwards to the mission fields. As evidence of the success of their missionary efforts, it suffices to say that when Bishop Juan de la Cabezas de Altamirano of Santiago, Cuba, visited Florida in 1606, he confirmed more than a thousand Indians.[11]

During the sixteenth century, the Franciscans had concentrated their missionary efforts primarily in Guale and in the eastern part of Timucua.[12] The seventeenth century found the members of the order advancing farther into Timucua province (the region around present-day Gainesville) and establishing contact with Apalachee province (the region around present-day Tallahassee).[13] Father Martín Prieto rendered signal service in the Franciscan advance into western Florida. He visited the Timucuan towns in 1607 and in the following year established contact with the Apalachee Indians.[14] Father Francisco Pareja stands out also in this westward advance. Arriving in Florida in 1595, he set to work and prepared a grammar and a dictionary in the Timucuan language as well as religious tracts.[15] Although missionary work had gone on in Timucua since 1565, Apalachee province did not receive a contingent of missionaries until 1633, when three Franciscans arrived to begin religious labors.[16]

The dedication of the Franciscans yielded results in the mission fields. Governor Damián Castro y Pardo (1638–1645) wrote to the king in 1639 that conversion of the Indians progressed at a good rate in Florida. He found this to be especially true in Apalachee, where, he asserted, that in spite of the fact that the province had only two padres, more than one thousand neophytes had been baptized. Emphasizing this figure, Castro requested that the crown send additional missionaries to Florida.[17] From time to time the neophytes rebelled and temporarily set the mission program back. Three Franciscans lost their lives in an Apalachee revolt in 1647. Governor Menéndez Marqués dealt severely with the insurgents. He executed several of the leaders and sentenced twenty-six Apalachees to work on the defensive fortifications at St. Augustine.[18]

The Timucuans revolted against Spanish authority in 1656 and enticed their Apalachee neighbors into joining them. Governor Diego de Rebolledo moved quickly to put down the uprising. Eleven malcontents were executed; and, by the end of 1657, the rebellious provinces had submitted again to Spanish dominion.

To insure against a future uprising, the Spanish governor stationed soldiers at San Luis.[19] In spite of inadequate supplies and the occasional rebellion of neophytes, the mission system flourished in Florida. The Franciscans could report in 1655 that 26,000 Indian converts lived in the *doctrinas* of Guale, Apalachee, and Timucua. And Bishop Gabriel Díaz Vara Calderón of Santiago, Cuba, confirmed 13,152 Indians and Spaniards in his ecclesiastical visitation to Guale, Apalachee, Timucua, and Apalachicola in 1674–1675.[20] The Franciscans enjoyed special success in Apalachee province, which numbered fourteen missions and several hundred Christianized Indians by 1680.[21] The mission system gave considerable stability to the Spanish frontier, and the crown continued to support it.[22]

Spanish activity did not confine itself solely to missionary and military matters in Florida. In 1648, Governor Benito Ruíz de Salazar attempted an agricultural experiment in Apalachee province, designed to remedy the food shortage that had existed almost from the time Menéndez founded the colony. The notoriously poor soil around St. Augustine had forced Spain to resort to a *situado* (subsidy) at an early date to maintain the garrison and the other colonists. Frequently, the subsidy arrived several years late. On numerous occasions, large portions of food had spoiled prior to delivery. The subsidy, even at its best, never satisfied the food requirements of Florida.[23] Governor Salazar knew that Panfilo de Narváez had noticed the fertility of Apalachee's soil in 1528. The governor knew also that Spanish vessels short of food had stopped for years at the Apalachee post of St. Marks to acquire cargoes of maize and wild turkeys.[24] Armed with this information, Governor Salazar ordered wheat planted in the province, and he sent to the Canary Islands for a miller. However, the governor died before the miller arrived, and his successors did not continue the agricultural project. Whether Apalachee wheat would have made Florida self-sufficient agriculturally is debatable, for the experiment in food production was not given a fair chance. It is interesting to note, however, that the Apalachee Indians grew sufficient quantities of the grain to end their dependence on St. Augustine for wheat.[25]

Failure of the wheat experiment in 1648 did not end Spanish interest in Apalachee province as a food-producing unit. Governor Hita Salazar, in 1675, wrote an interesting letter to the crown revealing his ideas for future development of the province. He stressed the superior fertility of the soil and advocated the importation of farmers to colonize the area. The colonists, in his opinion, would serve a double purpose. Increased agricultural development in Apalachee would make Florida more self-sufficient in food production and result in substantial savings to the crown. Also, the presence of a large number of colonists would act as a deterrent to English expansion from the Carolinas. The Florida governor suggested the Canary Islands as an excellent source from which to obtain colonists. Hita

Salazar pointed out also that there were navigable rivers flowing from Apalachee into the Gulf of Mexico, which would facilitate the transportation of food to St. Augustine. The governor strongly advocated that a stone fort, modeled after the Castillo de San Marcos at St. Augustine, be erected in the province to strengthen the Apalachee defensive system.[26]

Spain was firmly established in Florida by 1675. From the St. Augustine settlement of 1565 the Spanish had gone forward to erect a defensive system to protect their vessels sailing through the Bahama Channel. Simultaneously, Catholic fathers, principally Franciscans, had left the St. Augustine base to create a mission system in the provinces of Guale, Timucua, and Apalachee. Frequently the presidio stood alongside the mission on the Florida frontier. By 1675 the mission system had reached its zenith. At that particular time, the mission field stretched from near Charleston to the Gulf of Mexico, and the neophytes numbered several thousand.

Spain's control over most of the Southeast did not long remain uncontested. Sir Francis Drake had sacked St. Augustine in 1586, and England had followed Raleigh's failure at Roanoke Island with a successful colony at Jamestown. The Jamestown settlement alarmed Spanish authorities, but they decided to adopt a wait-and-see policy rather than to take affirmative measures to expel the new arrivals. This policy seemed satisfactory for the following half-century. During that time England was racked by civil war and other internal strife, and the Virginia colonists did not extend their holdings southward for any great distance.

When Charles II ascended the English throne in 1660, however, he made extensive land grants to his supporters, and many of them were in the region designated as Carolina. William Hilton explored the territory from Port Royal to Cape Fear in 1663, and three years later Robert Sandford led another expedition into the area. Sandford's visit was especially significant, for with him came Dr. Henry Woodward, a man destined to be the central figure in the English challenge to Spanish hegemony in the Southeast. When Sandford's expedition departed, the young doctor remained behind on the Carolina coast, applying himself immediately to learning Indian languages and the lay of the land. He soon appeared at St. Augustine, where he served as a physician to the town and the *castillo*. He remained there until 1668 when Robert Searles raided St. Augustine and took him away by force.[27] Woodward served as surgeon on Searles' ship for two years. On his return to Carolina in 1670, the knowledge he had previously gained in Spanish territory proved invaluable to the Charleston fur merchants when they extended their trade in the Georgia country after 1670.

In the Caribbean, the development of large sugar plantations based on slave labor forced many subsistence farmers to consider moving elsewhere. Barbados is an excellent case in point, for many of the economically displaced Barbadian farmers emigrated to the Carolinas where they helped to found the Charleston settlement in 1670. The establishment of this English base, in close proximity to St. Augustine, caused considerable concern to the Spanish authorities. As a naval base, Charleston presented a real threat to Spanish shipping through the Bahama Channel. The English settlement also served as a base from which fur traders could expand their activities into the interior. Before long, economic activities of the Carolina traders challenged Spain's influence over Indian groups, especially in present-day Georgia, for Woodward and his colleagues had inaugurated a determined effort to wrest the interior of the Southeast from Spanish control.[28]

The English had hardly settled Charleston when Henry Woodward visited the Indian village of Cufitachiqui near present-day Columbia, South Carolina.[29] Obviously impressed with the economic potential of the interior, he wrote to Sir John Yeamans, a Carolina proprietor, that the region appeared so "pleasant and fruitful, y^t were it cultivated it would prove a second Paradize." [30] While at Cufitachiqui, Woodward "contracted a league wth ye Empr and all those Petty Cassekas betwixt us and them." [31] The important Westo tribe, which blocked the way to the interior of Georgia, needed to be wooed in order for the inland fur trade to develop. This powerful Indian tribe intimidated the other Indians along the Savannah River. The Westos' reputation as cannibals enhanced other tribes' respect and fear of them.[32]

A delegation of Westo Indians visited Doctor Woodward in 1674. He accompanied them when they returned to their homes near the Savannah River because he had heard of rich stores of furs in that region. The fur trader stated upon reaching the villages, "haveing oyled my eyes and joynts with beares oyl, they presented mee divers deare skins, setting befoore me sufficient of their food to satisfy at least half a dozen of their owne appetites." [33] Impressed with the relative strength of the Westos, Woodward wrote that they were "well provided with arms, amunition, tradeing cloath and other trade from the northward for which at set times of the year they truck drest deare skins, furrs and young Indian slaves." [34] Ten of the Westos accompanied Doctor Woodward when he returned to Charleston; he sent them home and awaited their return in March 1675, when he hoped they would bring skins, furs, and Indian slaves to trade.[35] Woodward's diplomacy with the Westos succeeded, for their alliance with the Carolinians formed the basis of South Carolina's Indian policy from 1674 to 1680.[36] While Henry Woodward and other Carolina fur merchants occupied themselves with Indian diplomacy in eastern Georgia, Spanish officials worked hard in northern Florida and western Georgia—especially in Apalachee—to develop Indian alliances.

By 1680, however, the English settlers and the Westos were at odds. The lords proprietors of Carolina scolded the governor and council for allowing the alliance to weaken. Getting to the heart of the matter, the proprietors pointed out that friendship with the Westos would have kept other Indian tribes subdued. They noted further that the colonists could have protected the weaker tribes from Westo domination, and had they done so, the Carolina colony might have played a dominant role in intertribal rivalries.[37] On February 21, 1680, Andrew Percival departed for the Carolinas under instructions from the proprietors to negotiate a new treaty with the Westos.[38]

Apparently the excessive zeal of the Charleston fur merchants and slave-traders had precipitated the conflict with the Westos. On March 7, 1680, the proprietors wrote to the governor and council that if the Westo War was necessary for defense of the colony they condoned it; but if it had been started "to serve the ends of p[ar]ticular men we cannot but take it extremely ill that wee and the whole collony have been disturbed and putt in danger by a Warr to promote the advantage of particular persons." [39] Efforts were made to restore the alliance system, but ended in failure. When the Westos launched an attack against the coastal Edistoe Indians, the Carolinians, with the aid of the Shawnees, soundly defeated them. The remnants of the once powerful tribe then moved into the interior of the Georgia country and settled near the Ocmulgee River.[40] Not even a hundred Westos could be counted in 1683.[41]

While the Carolinians were engaged in decimating the Westos and opening the way into the Georgia country, the Spanish moved north up the Chattahoochee River and prepared to resist westward movement of the English. When Henry Woodward visited the Westos in 1674, the Apalachicola Indians,[42] possibly afraid that the English would advance into their area, asked Spain to send missionaries to their villages. The Franciscan fathers, however, could not fulfill the Apalachicola request until 1679, when they traveled up the Chattahoochee to establish a mission at Sabácola (near present-day Columbus, Georgia).[43] Emperor Brim, Chief of the Cowetas,[44] a powerful member of the Apalachicola confederacy, expelled the padres. The Franciscans returned in 1681 in the company of soldiers and established a mission, Santa Cruz de Sabácola, near the confluence of the Chattahoochee and Flint Rivers.[45] While the Franciscans labored to establish the Apalachicola mission, Dr. Woodward prepared to lead the Charleston fur traders across interior Georgia, and in 1685 he reached the banks of the Chattahoochee. Woodward's arrival in western Georgia precipitated an intensive Spanish effort to capture him and his followers. Governor Juan Marqués Cabrera (1680–1687) sent additional troops to reinforce the Apalachee presidio at San Luis and dispatched Lt. Antonio de Matheos up the Chattahoochee River in several futile attempts to capture the English intruders. The Apalachicolas, obviously impressed with superior English trade goods such as guns and ammunition, concealed Doctor Woodward and his followers from the Spanish. Matheos succeeded in confiscating trade goods and furs that belonged to the Carolina traders; and he burned the villages, Caveta, Tasquique, Casista and Colone, in an abortive effort to force the Apalachicolas to hand over the English.[46]

Doctor Woodward left the Chattahoochee in 1686 to return to Charleston, carried on a litter by Apalachicola porters because he was too ill to walk. Guale Indians, allied to Spain, attacked the small band of traders near the coast, killing four of them and capturing a large number of pelts. It is not clear whether Woodward himself died in the Georgia forest along with others of his party, but such a fate is suggested by the fact that Mrs. Woodward remarried in 1690.[47]

While pursuing the English fur traders, Lieutenant Matheos had left spies among the Apalachicolas to inform him if the English returned to the Chattahoochee. Soon afterwards the agents reported that the English traders had returned. Supposedly, Apalachicola braves, while hunting on the Pedernales (Flint) River, had encountered strange men. The village cacique related the information to the spies, who rushed the news to San Luis. Matheos dispatched the spies' reports to St. Augustine, although he was skeptical of them. He suspected that the cacique had issued false reports of English activity in an effort to get a Spanish insignia placed in his village as a symbol of protection.[48]

The punitive expeditions of Lieutenant Matheos caused considerable discontent among the Apalachicola Indians. When Governor Diego de Quiroga y Losada (1687–1693) visited Apalachee province in 1687, a delegation of Indians there complained bitterly to him about the destruction that Matheos had wreaked on their villages. They declared to Quiroga that Lieutenant Matheos had burned four of their large towns because they had given aid and cover to the English intruders of 1685. They expressed their belief, however, that the Spanish would help repair the damage. Governor Quiroga assured the Apalachicolas that Spain valued their friendship. In an effort to soothe Indian discontent, he assisted the Apalachicolas in solving their resettlement problems and in reviving the trade in agricultural produce and animal skins the Apalachicolas had formerly had with the Apalachees. Relieved that the Apalachicolas had apparently not become staunch allies of the English, Quiroga wrote:

> now, Your Grace, they [The Apalachicolas] remain calm and sure of their good treatment, and [they are] communicable with all, of which I report to Your Majesty, and of the said burning so felt by those poor Indians, it was a great providence of God that in revenge of their grievance they did not unite with the enemy from San Jorge [Charleston] and devastate our country, as the Yamasee Nation has done.[49]

Although Henry Woodward never returned to the Chattahoochee, other Carolina fur merchants such as Anthony Dodsworth and Thomas Nairne followed along the trail of trade he had blazed.[50] Spanish authorities, fully aware that these English intrusions jeopardized their control over western Georgia and Florida, decided to put an end to the Carolina fur trade on the Chattahoochee. Governor Quiroga, upon receiving a report from Lt. Francisco Romo de Uriza that the English had returned to Apalachicola, announced plans to build a presidio and to station infantrymen in the province to keep the English traders away from the Indians.[51] Administrative officials pointed out to the governor the difficulty of maintaining a garrison so far away from established posts.[52] Quiroga, however, persisted in his determination and soon afterwards dispatched Captain Primo de Rivera and twenty-four infantrymen to Apalachicola to construct a fortress. Rivera was chosen to supervise construction of the *casa fuerte* because of his experience with fortifications while serving in Flanders. Governor Quiroga sent a hundred Indians, many of whom were carpenters, with Captain Rivera so that the fort could be completed within two months.[53]

The finished fortress, complete with bastions and moat, was structurally similar to the Castillo de San Marcos at St. Augustine.[54] The blockhouse measured 22 *varas* (61.16 feet) on the north to south side and 19 *varas* (52.82 feet) on the east to west side. The parapet, or outside elevation to protect soldiers, measured 1.5 *varas* (4.18 feet) in thickness. The moat that surrounded the fort measured 4 *varas* (11.12 feet) in width.[55] Two plans of Fort Apalachicola are extant. One shows the stockade, moat, plaza, main entrance, sallyport, and the bastions.[56] The other deals primarily with the interior of the *casa fuerte*, but includes the moat, stockade, plaza, storerooms, and barracks for the soldiers. It does not include the bastions and sallyport.[57] Fort Apalachicola was structurally similar to the St. Augustine *castillo*, the principal difference being in the type of materials used.[58]

Lt. Fabián de Angulo traveled up the Chattahoochee River in the spring of 1690 to assume command of the garrison. Angulo reported on April 14 that he had taken command of the fort, and that the garrison consisted of a corporal, two *reformados* (officers deprived of former commands), and seventeen regular soldiers. He noted also that there were twenty Apalachee Indians who would serve as laborers in the *casa fuerte*. The supply of weapons and munitions appeared adequate to Angulo. In an emergency he knew that the garrison could quickly obtain additional supplies of men and material from San Luis.[59]

At Fort Apalachicola, Lieutenant Angulo did what he could to maintain friendly relations with the Indians. He gave them seed corn to plant their fields and promised to supply them from the garrison stores if they should need food in the interim. At Caveta, Angulo told the Apalachicolas that they had erred in trading with the English. In reply, the Indians explained that the English had supplied them with guns, munitions, and other needed articles, and that they had paid for the trade items with animal skins. Angulo told the Apalachicolas that the garrison had been placed in their province to protect them from the English and from hostile Indians who might come into the area. He insisted that they must not trade with the English and that they must report to him if the English resumed trading in their villages. The garrison commander put the question of allegiance squarely to the Apalachicolas, and they affirmed their loyalty to Spain.[60] No doubt many of these Indians remembered that their reception of Woodward had resulted in the destruction that Antonio de Matheos dealt them in 1686.

With the building of the fortress on the Chattahoochee in 1689 and the strengthening of its garrison the following year, Spain seemed to have gained the upper hand over her European rival. The success proved to be short-lived, however, for the fortress lost its importance after less than a year. The Apalachicola Indians were convinced that the Spanish garrison would prevent the English fur merchants from returning to the Chattahoochee. This meant the loss of their source of English trade items, which were of superior quality and more abundant than those available from the Spanish. Probably influenced by this situation, most of the Apalachicolas left the Chattahoochee to relocate on the Ocmulgee River in central Georgia. Fort Apalachicola no longer served a useful purpose. With the departure of most of the Indians, the *casa fuerte* seemed to be a useless drain on the treasury of Florida. The ultimate decision regarding the fortress was also affected by events taking place in other areas of the Spanish empire.

In 1691, Juan de la Fuente testified before a junta in Havana that French pirates had heard about the weakened condition of St. Augustine, and were planning to attack the town. Authorities in Havana notified Governor Quiroga of the impending assault, and the governor immediately sought means to strengthen the St. Augustine presidio.[61] No support from outside sources was forthcoming; therefore, men and supplies would have to be brought from other sections of Florida. Quiroga declined to withdraw troops from Guale because of its proximity to Carolina. Nor did he wish to reduce the Apalachee garrison because that area was also subject to pirate raids. He hesitated to recall soldiers from Timucua, for towns in that region had recently been destroyed by the English and their Uchise and Yamasee Indian allies. He then turned his attention to the garrison at Fort Apalachicola as a possible solution to the manpower shortage at the St. Augustine presidio. Knowing that most of the Apalachicolas had left the Chattahoochee, Quiroga decided to order the demolition of the fort and the return of its garrison to St. Augustine.[62] On September 18, 1691, a junta met in St. Augustine and voted unanimously to accept the governor's plan.[63]

Governor Quiroga dispatched an order to Lt. Patricio de Florencia to demolish the fort, fill the moat, and render the site useless for military purposes. Florencia was instructed to remove arms, munitions, food, and anything else that might be of service to the enemy. At the same time, Florencia was to invite the Apalachicolas to reoccupy their former villages, provided, of course, that they would not continue commercial relations with the English.[64] Lieutenant Florencia and the garrison carried out the governor's instructions, then departed from the Chattahoochee to reinforce the presidio at St. Augustine.

Fort Apalachicola represents, in retrospect, a kind of high-water mark of Spanish expansion in the Georgia country during the seventeenth century. The Anglo-Spanish rivalry involved missionaries, soldiers, and traders, but the Indians were the central issue. Spain's Indian policy was conducted primarily by the padres and soldiers, while that of England was carried out principally by men of commercial interests. Spanish expeditions sent to stop the English intruders failed mainly because the Indians desired English trade goods. The construction of Fort Apalachicola, while designed to undermine the English influence, actually enhanced it. The movement by the Apalachicola Indians in the direction of Charleston, followed by the withdrawal of the Spanish garrison, seems to indicate a victory for England in the field of Indian diplomacy. This victory helped prepare the way for the establishment of the colony of Georgia by James Oglethorpe in the following century.

Notes

1. Paul Quattlebaum, *The Land Called Chicora* (Gainesville: University of Florida Press, 1956), pp. 18–27.

2. Herbert Eugene Bolton, *The Spanish Borderlands* (New Haven: Yale University Press, 1921), pp. 128–33.

3. Jean Ribaut, *The Whole and true discouerye of Terra Florida;* a facsimile reprint of the London edition of 1563, together with a transcript of an English version in the British museum with notes by H. M. Biggar, and a bibliography by Jeannette Thurber Connor (De Land: The Florida State Historical Society, 1927), pp. 58–97; and Bolton, *The Spanish Borderlands,* pp. 136–137.

4. Gonzalo Solís de Merás, *Pedro Menéndez de Avilés, Adelantado Governor and Captain-General of Florida,* trans. Jeannette Thurber Connor (De Land: The Florida State Historical Society, 1923), pp. 74–104.

5. The Guale Indians lived in the province that extended along the Georgia coast from the "Savannah River as far as St. Andrews Sound."

See John R. Swanton, *Early History of the Creek Indians and Their Neighbors* (Washington, D.C.: Bureau of American Ethnology, Bulletin 73, 1922), p. 80.

6. Mary Ross, "With Pardo and Boyano on the Fringes of the Georgia Land," *Georgia Historical Quarterly*, (December 1930), vol. 14 p. 283. (hereinafter cited as *G.H.Q.*); and Report of the Entry and Conquest Made by Order of Pedro Menéndez de Avilés in 1565 into the interior of Florida by Juan Pardo, trans. Herbert E. Ketcham, in "Three Sixteenth Century Spanish Chronicles Relating to Georgia," *G.H.Q.*, (March 1954), vol. 38, p. 69.

7. Michael V. Gannon, *The Cross in the Sand: The Early Catholic Church in Florida 1513–1870* (Gainesville: University of Florida Press, 1965), pp. 32–34; Herbert Eugene Bolton and Mary Ross, *The Debatable Land* (Berkeley: University of California Press, 1925), p. 10; and Clifford M. Lewis and Albert J. Loomíe, *The Spanish Jesuit Mission in Virginia 1570–1577* (Chapel Hill: University of North Carolina Press, 1953), pp. 28, 45.

8. Gannon, *Cross in the Sand*, p. 39. Father Gannon states that the Franciscan *doctrina* was "A mission where there was a resident friar."

9. In Guale the term *mico* was synonymous with that of cacique or chief, and apparently there was a *mico* who exercised a degree of influence over the entire province. See Swanton, *Early History of the Creek Indians*, p. 84.

10. Tolomato was located across from Sapelo Island on the Georgia mainland. Bolton and Ross, *The Debatable Land*, p. 15.

11. John Tate Lanning, *The Spanish Missions of Georgia* (Chapel Hill: University of North Carolina Press, 1935), pp. 82–109; J. G. Johnson, "The Yamasee Revolt of 1597 and the Destruction of the Georgia Missions," *G.H.Q.*, (March, 1923), vol. 7, pp. 46–50; Mary Ross, "The Restoration of the Spanish Missions In Georgia, 1598–1606," *G.H.Q.* (September, 1926), vol. 10, pp. 174–85; and Gannon, *Cross in the Sand*, pp. 46–47.

12. David I. Bushnell, Jr., *Native Village Sites East of the Mississippi* (Washington, D.C.: Bureau of American Ethnology, Bulletin 69, 1919), pp. 15, 89. Bushnell defines Timucua as an area extending from St. Augustine west to the Aucilla River and down the Gulf Coast to Tampa. See also Swanton, *Early History of the Creek Indians*, pp. 320–30.

13. Apalachee province centered around present-day Tallahassee, Florida. It was limited principally by the Aucilla River on the east and the Ocklocknee River and its tributaries to the west. Swanton, *Early History of the Creek Indians*, p. 110.

14. Gannon, *Cross in the Sand*, p. 51.

15. Ibid., pp. 52–54.

16. Lanning, *Spanish Missions of Georgia*, p. 166.

17. Carta a S.M. de Damian de la Vega Castro y Pardo Sobre Varios Asuntos de la Florida, August 22, 1639, in Manuel Serrano y Sanz, ed., *Documentos Historicos De La Florida y La Luisiana. Siglos XVI al XVIII* (Madrid: Biblioteca de los Americanistas), p. 198.

18. Lanning, *Spanish Missions of Georgia*, p. 168; Gannon, *Cross in the Sand*, p. 56.

19. Ibid., p. 169. San Luis, located near Tallahassee, Florida, has been excavated. An excellent report has been written about the site by John W. Griffin of the National Park Service, which is to be found in Mark F. Boyd, Hale G. Smith, and John W. Griffin, *Here They Once Stood: The Tragic End of The Apalachee Missions* (Gainesville: University of Florida Press, 1951), pp. 139–58.

20. *A Seventeenth Century Letter of Gabriel Díaz Vara Calderón, Bishop of Cuba, Describing the Indians and Indian Missions of Florida*, trans. Lucy L. Wenhold, in Smithsonian Miscellaneous Collections (Washington, D.C., 1936), vol. 95, p. 12.

21. Don Pablo de Hita Salazar to the Queen, in trans. Mark F. Boyd, "Enumeration of Florida Spanish Missions in 1675," *Florida Historical Quarterly*, (October 1948), vol. 27, pp. 184–186 (hereinafter cited as *F.H.Q.*).

22. Herbert E. Bolton, "The Mission as a Frontier Institution in the Spanish-American Colonies," *American Historical Review*, (October 1917), vol. 23, p. 47 (hereinafter cited as *A.H.R.*).

23. Verne Elmo Chatelaine, *The Defenses of Spanish Florida 1565–1763* (Washington, D.C.: Carnegie Institution Publication 511, 1941), p. 9.

24. Bolton and Ross, *The Debatable Land*, p. 26.

25. Katherine S. Lawson, "Governor Salazar's Wheat Farm Project 1647–1657," *F.H.Q.* (January 1946), vol. 24, pp. 196–200.

26. Don Pablo de Hita Salazar to the King, in trans. Katherine Reding, "Plans for the Colonization and Defense of Apalachee, 1675," *G.H.Q.* (June 1926), vol. 9, pp. 169–71. Salazar mentioned in his report to the crown the threat not only of English aggression but also of French. He stated that the French had established a settlement on the Gulf of Mexico. In 1675, France did not have an outpost or colony on the Gulf.

27. Irene A. Wright, "Spanish Policy Toward Virginia 1606–1612; Jamestown, Ecija and John Clark of the Mayflower," *A.H.R.*, (April 1920), vol. 25, pp. 449–78; William Hilton, "A True Relation of a Voyage upon discovery of part of the Coast of Florida, from the Lat. of 31 Deg. to 33 Deg. 45 m. North Lat. in the ship adventure, William Hilton Commander and Commissioner with Captain Anthony Long and Peter Fabian set forth by several Gentlemen and Merchants of the Island of Barbadoes; sailed from Spikes Bay Aug. 10 1663," in *Collections of the South Carolina Historical Society*, (Richmond: William Ellis Jones, 1897), vol. 5, p. 26; Robert Sandford, "A Relation of a Voyage on the Coast of the Province of Carolina, Formerly Called Florida, in the Continent of the Northern America, from Charles River near Cape Feare, in the County of Clarendon, and the Lat. of 34 Deg: to Port Royal, in the North Lat: of 32 Deg: begun 14th June, 1666; Performed by Robert Sandford, Esque, Secretary and Chiefe Register for the Lords Proprietors of their County of Clarendon, in the Province Aforesaid," in *Narratives of Early Carolina 1650–*

1708, ed. Alexander Samuel Salley, Jr. (New York: Charles Scribner's Sons, 1911), p. 105; and Bolton and Ross, *The Debatable Land,* p. 31.

28. Edward McCrady, *The History of South Carolina Under the Proprietary Government 1670–1719* (New York: Macmillan Company, 1897), vol. 1, p. 129; Verner W. Crane, *The Southern Frontier 1670–1732* (Durham: Duke University Press, 1928), p. 10; and Governor Manuel de Cendoya to the crown, Mar. 24, 1672, trans. José Miguel Gallardo, "The Spaniards and the English Settlement in Charles Town," *South Carolina Historical and Genealogical Magazine,* (April 1936), vol. 37, p. 50 (hereinafter cited as *S.C.H.G.M.*).

29. Mary Ross locates Cufitachiqui near Columbia, S.C. See Mary Ross, "With Pardo and Boyano on the Fringes of the Georgia Land," *G.H.Q.,* (December, 1930), vol. 14, p. 273.

30. H. Woodward to Sir John Yeamans, Sept. 10, 1670, *Collections of the South Carolina Historical Society,* (Richmond: William Ellis Jones, 1897), vol. 5, p. 186.

31. Ibid, p. 187.

32. Swanton, *Early History of the Creek Indians,* p. 66.

33. Henry Woodward, "A Faithfull Relation of my Westoe Voiage" (1674), in *Narratives of Early Carolina 1650–1708,* ed. Alexander S. Salley, Jr. (New York: Charles Scribner's Sons, 1911), p. 133.

34. Ibid., p. 133.

35. Ibid., p. 134.

36. Crane, *The Southern Frontier,* p. 17.

37. *Records in the British Public Record Office Relating to South Carolina, 1663–1710,* indexed by Alexander S. Salley, Jr. (Atlanta: Foote and Davies Company, 1928–1947), vol. 1, p. 104 (hereinafter cited as *Records B.P.R.O.*).

38. *Records B.P.R.O.,* vol. 1, p. 106.

39. Ibid., p. 115.

40. Swanton, *Early History of the Creek Indians,* p. 307.

41. *Records B.P.R.O.,* vol. 1, p. 112.

42. Apalachicola refers generally to Lower Creek towns. See Swanton, *Early History of the Creek Indians,* p. 129.

43. Bolton and Ross, *The Debatable Land,* p. 47. Bolton and Ross locate Sabácola on the Chattahoochee River a few miles below the falls near present-day Columbus, Georgia. Apalachicola was the Spanish term for Lower Creeks.

44. Coweta was the foremost war town among the Apalachicolas. Swanton, *Early History of the Creek Indians,* p. 133.

45. Bolton and Ross, *The Debatable Land,* p. 48.

46. Matheos to Cabrera, Sept. 21, 1685; Domingo de Leturiondo to Cabrera, Nov. 5, 1685, Archivo General de Indias, 58-1-26 (hereinafter cited as *A.G.I.*). Matheos to Cabrera, Jan. 12, 1686; Matheos to Cabrera, Feb. 8, 1686; Matheos to Cabrera, Mar. 14, 1686; and Cabrera to the viceroy, Mar. 19, 1686, *A.G.I.* 58-4-23.

47. Cabrera to the King, Nov. 8, 1686, *A.G.I.* 54-5-12. See also Joseph W. Barnwell, "Doctor Henry Woodward the First English Settler in

South Carolina and Some of His Descendants" *S.C.H.G.M.*, (January 1907), vol. 8, p. 103.

48. Carta del Teniente de Apalache, Antonio Matheos al Señor Gobernador y Capitán-General da La Florida, Acerca de Haber Vuelto Los Ingleses a La Provincia de Apalachicoli, San Luis, 19 de Mayo de 1606 [*sic*, 1686] in Serrano Y Sanz, ed., *Documentos Históricos*, p. 195.

49. Carta a S.M. del Governador de San Agustín de la Florida Don Diego de Quiroga, San Agustín, 10 de Abril de 1688 in Serrano Y Sanz, ed., *Documentos Históricos*, p. 220.

50. Crane, *The Southern Frontier*, pp. 43–46.

51. Quiroga to the king, Sept. 29, 1689, *A.G.I.* 54-5-12.

52. Fort Apalachicola was 160 leagues from St. Augustine and 80 leagues from Apalachee province. See Autto Sobre aver Mandado retirar la Guarnicion de Apalachecolo, Quiroga to the king, Apr. 10, 1692, *A.G.I.* 54-5-13.

53. Quiroga to the king, June 8, 1690, *A.G.I.* 54-5-12.

54. See Figure A. Enclosure in Quiroga to the king, June 8, 1690, *A.G.I.* 54-5-12.

55. Angulo to Quiroga, Apr. 14, 1690, *A.G.I.* 54-5-12. See also "Two Early Letters from Alabama," ed. Mark E. Fretwell, *The Alabama Review* (January, 1956), vol. 9, pp. 54–65. Fretwell includes translations of Angulo's letters to Quiroga of Apr. 14 and May 24, 1690. I have accepted Fretwell's English equivalents of the *vara* measurements of Ft. Apalachicola.

56. Figure A. Enclosure in Quiroga to the king, June 8, 1690, *A.G.I.* 54-5-12.

57. Figure B., *A.G.I.* 54-5-12.

58. Fretwell, in "Two Early Letters from Alabama," p. 65, suggested that the probable location for the fort was near Holy Trinity in Russell County, Ala. Brother Finbar, of the Trinitarian mission in the area, found what appeared to be the site. The University of Alabama excavated the site in the summer of 1962. Professor Lewis Larson of Georgia State College directed a combined crew of University of Alabama and Florida State students in the excavation under the overall supervision of Professor David L. DeJarnette of the University of Alabama. Edward Kurjack, a graduate student of Professor DeJarnette, wrote the report on the site designated as 1 Ru 101. Kurjack's report will be published in "Archaeological Salvage in the Walter F. George Basin of the Chattahoochee Valley in Alabama," ed. David L. DeJarnette. Kurjack concluded, on the basis of excavated structural features and recovered artifacts, both Indian and Spanish, that the site could be Fort Apalachicola. The excavation revealed that a wattle and daub type of construction was used for the Spanish fort.

59. Angulo to Quiroga, Apr. 14, 1690, *A.G.I.* 54-5-12.

60. Angulo to Quiroga, May 24, 1690, *A.G.I.* 54-5-12.

61. Declaracion por donde consta estar el enemego frances con disignios de benir a apresar este presidio de la florida, Quiroga to the king, Apr. 10, 1692, *A.G.I.* 54-5-12.

62. Autto Sobre aver Mandado retirar la Guarnicion de Apalachicola, Quiroga to the king, Apr. 10, 1692, *A.G.I.* 54–5–12.

63. Junta, Quiroga to the king, Apr. 10, 1692, *A.G.I.* 54–5–12.

64. Horden para Retirar la Guarnicion de Apalachocole, Quiroga to the king, Apr. 10, 1692, *A.G.I.* 54–5–12.

2 | Anglo-Spanish Negotiations Involving Central America in 1783

Conwell A. Anderson

Anglo-Spanish relations in Central America began about 1660, and were characterized by resentment, misunderstanding, overt hostilities, and temporary treaties. The principal points at issue involved territorial rights and the cutting and transporting of logwood. Although the logwood tree grew throughout Central America, the Spanish at first centered their cutting in the vicinity of the Bay of Campeche; for this reason, the wood was sometimes referred to as campeche wood. After the supply in this area was exhausted, the Spanish logwood cutters pushed into the area around the Gulf of Honduras. This region soon became the center of Spanish operations.

English logwood cutters moved into the vicinity of the Gulf of Honduras in the second half of the seventeenth century. The Spanish tolerated their presence for a time, but they soon came to realize that the English entrepreneurs presented a territorial as well as a commercial threat. Therefore, in the early eighteenth century the Spanish attempted, through diplomacy and military force, to expel the foreigners, but their efforts ended in failure.

The Peace of Paris, signed in 1763 was an important event in the contest for control of the Central American coast. Article 17 of that document stated that all British fortifications in the area had to be demolished, but it allowed Britishers to live there and to continue cutting logwood.[1] Many British merchants engaged in colonial trade at the time interpreted this article to mean that Great Britain had no legal claim to the area and that Spain was merely tolerating the presence of British logwood cutters.[2] Vera L. Brown, an authority on British colonial affairs, does not concur, but contends that Great Britain "compelled the recognition of the legality of the presence of the British logwood cutters in Honduras Bay."[3] England and Spain continued to debate the meaning of Article 17 for some years. Finally, Spain's participation in the war of the American Revolution as an enemy of Great Britain brought the boundary question back into the diplomatic negotiations designed to end that struggle.

As peace negotiations progressed in Paris during 1782, Spain demanded the evacuation of British settlers and cutters from the entire region of Honduras. On December 16, Great Britain presented a counter proposition that provided for preservation of her logwood cutting privileges, limited by certain restrictions. The Spanish ambassador, Pedro Pablo Abarca, conde de Aranda, stated that he did not have the authority to agree to any stipulation that would entitle the British to cut logwood, regardless of what restrictions were involved and that he would have to seek approval from Madrid.[4] At this point in the negotiations, Aranda dispatched his secretary, Ignacio de Heredia, to London to facilitate discussion while he sought further authorization and instructions from Madrid. In London, Heredia maintained that all British settlements had to be evacuated, but Sir Thomas Robinson, second baron Grantham, the secretary of state for colonial affairs, insisted that it was impossible for Britain to give up the privileges recognized in 1763.[5] Alleyne Fitzherbert, British minister plenipotentiary in Paris, concurred and convinced Aranda that the presence of British cutters had to be tolerated, but their area of operations could be specifically defined.

When the proposal of December 16 had been reported back to Madrid and approved, Aranda agreed to Article 4 of a preliminary treaty, which stated that Spain would "not allow . . . any British subjects to be disturbed . . . in cutting . . . logwood or campeche wood in a district, the boundaries of which . . . would be fixed." [6] Fitzherbert signed the treaty for Great Britain.

The signing represented a distinct diplomatic and strategic victory for Spain. Throughout the negotiations, Aranda had insisted on both the elimination of the British from the Caribbean and the retrocession of Gibraltar. Together they were unreasonable demands, but defense policy dictated one and public opinion the other. However, as soon as Great Britain offered to meet most of the Spanish demands involving the Caribbean and agreed to restrictions on the rest—in exchange for Spain's giving up her claim to Gibraltar—Aranda accepted immediately. Realistically, the Spanish ministry knew it could never obtain all of its demands. When those involving defense policy were met, the others were withdrawn. Historians have assumed that

Spain would have been willing to agree to extensive sacrifices for the return of Gibraltar. However, there is no proof of this. On the contrary, the documents indicate that the Spaniards considered their Caribbean holdings of greater value than Gibraltar and very adeptly used the Rock as a pawn in the negotiations.[7] This article deals with the details of the negotiations that followed the signing of the preliminary treaty, as each country struggled to interpret Article 4 to its advantage and satisfaction.

Before negotiations were continued, Fitzherbert informed Aranda that his government expected that British settlers along the entire coast would be unmolested until the district limits were drawn up, and that proper time would be given later for them to move within the district or elsewhere. Aranda agreed and signed a declaration to that effect.[8]

Instructions arriving from José de Gálvez, minister of the Indies, became the basis upon which the Spanish negotiators justified their unyielding attitude in subsequent weeks. In these directives, Gálvez authorized Aranda to agree that British logwood-cutting activities be restricted to one clearly defined, sixty-mile district between the New and Belize Rivers. The English were to evacuate the rest of the Central American coast.[9]

Fitzherbert's instructions to persuade Aranda to consider additional areas delayed negotiations in early 1783. When it became apparent that Aranda was adamant, Britain agreed to restrict discussions to the New–Belize River district as Gálvez had instructed Aranda.[10] In a letter of March 4 Aranda explained in detail to Fitzherbert the extent of this district and proposed that the two rivers be used in common by the Spanish and English logwood cutters. The district bounded by these rivers provided a region of about eleven hundred square miles, which in Aranda's opinion contained the best quality of logwood. He further reminded Fitzherbert of the many excellent harbors which would facilitate transportation from any part of the district.[11]

Fitzherbert immediately sent this offer to Grantham in London, observing, however, that the proposed district provided a rather scanty supply of logwood, which might not last for long. He also felt that the location was not satisfactory because none of the British settlements already in the area were within the proposed limits. For these reasons he felt certain that his government would consider the proposals inadequate. To these objections Aranda replied that in accordance with Article 4, Spain would consider any offer that London made in good faith either to extend the boundaries or to transfer the entire district.[12] Upon receipt of the Spanish offer and Fitzherbert's comments, Grantham assured Fitzherbert that his observations and attitude were entirely just and that he, Grantham, also felt that the Spanish proposals were unacceptable.[13]

As the British ministry considered the proposal, a new Spanish representative, Don Bernardo de Campo, arrived to replace Heredia, who rejoined Aranda's staff in Paris. En route to London, Campo stopped at Paris and assured Aranda of support by the crown. In London, Campo was recognized as a minister plenipotentiary with a broader scope of authority than that exercised by Heredia, although his chief function was to serve as a source of information for Aranda, who was continuing the primary negotiations in Paris.[14]

To find grounds for demanding a larger district and to gain a clearer understanding of the local situation, the British foreign ministry sought information from the English settlers and merchants who had been driven out by the Spaniards in 1779. At the same time they informed Campo that no reply or decision would be made on the basis of the inadequate information the ministry had on hand.[15] The settlers and merchants complied with a comprehensive memorial written by their agent Robert White, which undoubtedly influenced the British ministry considerably. The attitude of the authors of this memorial toward Aranda's proposal was one of contempt; they were convinced that Spain's purpose was to make any further British settlements impractical. Therefore, they presented a survey of the entire region that the British settlers considered to be "their area." They did not mention the length of time they had occupied the land, but interpreted the 1763 Treaty of Paris as assigning to Great Britain the entire region from the South Monkey River,[16] north to Cape Cartouche in Yucatan. They also claimed that they had occupied and cut logwood from the Manatee Lagoon on the south to the Hondo River on the north, concentrating on the areas of the New River, Rowley's Bight, the Northern River, and the Sibun River. They insisted that if any part of the coast had to be sacrificed it should be the badly cutover Hondo River region. This area was of little strategic value to the British but of considerable worth to the Spaniards, for it provided an entrance to the province and town of Bacalar, twelve miles upstream.[17]

As for the operations to the South, White observed that the area from the Sibun River to the Manatee Lagoon could also be surrendered because of lack of logwood. However, mahogany had recently been discovered in the area and might be more valuable than logwood, since the market for the latter faced a possible price reduction. Accordingly, he urged against an unwitting sacrifice of this potentially valuable region.[18]

To avoid future misunderstandings, the memorialists reminded the ministry that the treaty should include a clear statement recognizing the right of British fishermen and turtlers to navigate and occupy "all or any of the quays or islands along the coast, which lie or are situated to the westward of a line drawn from Cape Gracias a Dios to Cape Cartouche." [19] They emphasized the need to have this right acknowledged because the fishermen and turtlers provided the main source of food for the loggers. They further reminded the ministry that there would be no need to extend the proposed line from Cape Gracias a Dios, which was at the eastern point of the Mosquito Coast, if the British did not acknowledge Spain's sovereignty in that region. They appear to have accepted Spanish ownership of the area while pressing for a guarantee of the privilege of occupation. Writing more specifically, they asked for a definite recognition of their right to occupy and build homes on the islands of St. George and on the group known as the Southern Triangles, along with any other islands located opposite the district, which they expected would eventually extend to the Manatee Lagoon.

Inasmuch as the British government had agreed to restrict their operations to a definite district, White offered specific suggestions. He proposed that the British ministry offer to abandon claim to the region south of the South Monkey River in return for possession of any of the unoccupied eastern coast of Yucatan north of a point approximately forty miles north of the Hondo River.[20]

The memorial further suggested that if a war should break out between Great Britain and Spain, Spanish ships operating in the Gulf of Honduras would have a free period of six months during which to embark unmolested. British settlers in Honduras would have the same period in which to transfer their families, property, and effects out of the region.[21] This indicated that the British recognized the formidable extent of Spanish control in the Caribbean and acknowledged that the presence of the British was merely being tolerated.

Fitzherbert and Grantham had opposed the initial proposal of a district between the Belize and New Rivers. Aranda wrote Campo urging him to try to influence Charles James Fox, Grantham's successor as secretary of state for colonial affairs, to accept the arrangement. Aranda indicated that the district could only be expanded into the interior and then only with approval from the minister of the Indies. Campo wrote to Fox urging him to comply with the Spanish offer.[22]

Fox appeared to be more favorably inclined than Grantham had been. He told Campo that he needed more information on the quality and quantity of the logwood in the district offered them. He was also inclined to press for several districts rather than just one. Fox further suggested that the right to cut logwood might be stated in general terms in the definitive treaty, after which the district could be arranged carefully and without haste. Though Campo had assured him that the Spanish offer fixing the New and Belize Rivers as boundaries would never be enlarged, Fox suggested that the northern boundary be moved to the Hondo River. In reply, Campo observed that the suggestion had no sound basis, and, if accepted, it would be considered a personal victory for Fox rather than an indication of a generous Spanish spirit.[23]

As he sparred verbally with Campo, Fox received the White memorial from Honduras. After analyzing it, he send two propositions to Fitzherbert to present to Aranda as counterproposals to the latter's original offer. The first of these followed the suggestion of the Honduran settlers and appeared to give the British the entire coast. Fitzherbert set it aside as impractical. The second, however, he urged Aranda to accept. It proposed the Hondo River as the northern boundary and the South Monkey River as the southern. Aranda responded by assuring Fitzherbert that the initial offer of coastal boundaries at the Belize and New Rivers was the ultimatum of the Spanish court, though he offered to extend the district into the interior to provide an additional hundred square miles. Fitzherbert stated to Fox that he discerned in Aranda a disposition to extend the proposed border from the New to the Hondo River, but he saw no hope of any southern extension.[24]

After analyzing the negotiations, Fitzherbert contended that Aranda was being unreasonably stubborn on all points discussed, even to the extent of emphasizing his points with great heat and near violence.[25] Aranda's correspondence with Campo, however, shows that he was not blinded by stubbornness, for he suggested that they consider confidentially the possibility of enlarging the disct still farther into the interior to facilitate a settlement.[26] Yet he made no overt gesture of this nature to either Fitzherbert or Manchester, Fitzherbert's replacement in Paris, nor did he authorize Campo to make such a proposal to Fox.[27]

Charles Gravier, comte de Vergennes, who represented France in the peace negotiations, made an effort on May 21 to arrange a settlement by proposing that the district extend along the entire coast from Cape Cartouche south to the South Monkey River.[28] England, realizing Spain would never consider such a settlement, did not encourage Vergennes. The proposal is evidence that Vergennes did not grasp the significance of Spain's efforts to limit British activity as a part of a larger defense program.

The same day that Vergennes made his proposal to the British, Aranda sent a letter directly to Fox, reiterating Spain's attitude on Honduras. He emphasized that England's request for an enlargement of the original eleven hundred square-mile district had been met and that Spain was willing to enlarge it further to a proposed thirty-three hundred square miles, still between the New and Belize Rivers. He reminded Fox that the proposed district, with natural borders on three sides, would reduce the possibility of future friction, which might easily occur if the divisions were not distinctly marked by navigable rivers.[29]

Fox, remaining adamant, refused to accept the Spanish proposal; while Manchester, still anticipating that eventually both the northern and southern boundaries would be extended, continued to press the British counterproposal. Manchester informed Fox that although Aranda insisted that he was bound by the Spanish crown to accept no northern or southern boundary extensions, Manchester suspected that Aranda's authority was broader than he wished to admit. Thus the most effective approach would be one of continued discussion.

Manchester noted in the same letter that his maps did not show the Mullino River, which was mentioned as a possible boundary by the Honduras settlers, and indicated that he had taken the liberty of choosing the South Monkey River as the proposed limit, not realizing that the two names designated the same river.[30] A more comprehensive map was sent to him on June 10, 1783, together with instructions to continue to insist upon the South Monkey River as the southern boundary. If this was refused with finality, he was to request permission to cut wood along the Manatee Lagoon. As to the northern boundary, he was still to insist on the Hondo River. If none of these demands were met, Manchester was directed to insist upon a depth of at least ninety miles for the district as it was already defined. Since the distance between the New and Belize Rivers was sixty miles by Spanish calculation, this would mean fifty-four hundred square miles or about twice the amount Spain was offering. Fox closed his letter pessimistically, expressing doubt that they could ever persuade the Spanish to extend the boundaries beyond the New and Belize rivers.[31]

Manchester finally succeeded in obtaining a boundary extension from Aranda. After it was mutually understood that each man had full authority to conclude a treaty, Aranda convinced Manchester that no extension to the south was possible but that the northern coastal boundary could be set at the Hondo River. The two negotiators also agreed that the British territory should extend inland for a depth of seventy-five miles.[32]

The discussion next shifted to British rights outside of this specifically defined district. Aranda consented to allow the British settlers to fish along the coast of the district but not beyond its limits. The question of neighboring islands was then posed. In an earlier memorial, the British settlers had emphasized the need to obtain fishing rights on St. George and Roatan Islands. They had also stated that it was imperative to have permission to fortify them against a surprise attack.[33] John Dalling, in a letter to Viscount Montstuart, British ambassador to Spain, had emphasized that if the island of Roatan were not retained, none of the ceded area would be of any consequence to Great Britain.[34] Although Manchester pressed Aranda to grant these demands, the Spaniard stood firm; he consented to grant only the privilege of fishing from the islands and insisted on a specific reservation against building fortifications.[35] (Aranda's attitude was entirely in keeping with the overall defense program for the Caribbean. The extension from the New River to the Hondo River was of minor consequence compared with the larger objective of restricting the English to a defined district.) One additional agreement was reached which granted British settlers eighteen months in which to evacuate other settlements they had occupied on the continent or islands outside the defined district.[36]

In London, Campo informed Fox that these agreements meant that the British must limit their settlements to the defined region. Fox contended that this was a new and unacceptable interpretation of

Article 4 of the preliminary treaty, and he insisted upon occupational rights on the islands of St. George and the South Triangles.[37]

In subsequent weeks Great Britain tried to alter the interpretation of the agreement that Manchester and Aranda had drawn up. When Manchester questioned Aranda about the basis for the Spanish interpretation, Aranda reminded him that the preliminary treaty had stated specifically that the British were to be confined to one district.[38] Manchester realized that there could be no other logical explanation and informed Fox that the best conditions possible had been procured, though he realized that they would work a hardship on those settlers outside the defined district.[39] Not grasping the binding character of the agreement, Fox informed Manchester that evacuation of all settlements outside of the agreed-on district could not be accepted.[40] He wrote that he had not even considered this possibility when he had spoken to Fitzherbert, who was then in London. Fitzherbert had informed him that he had understood throughout the negotiations that the British would be expected to evacuate all other parts of the continent, including the Mosquito Coast. He had referred Fox to correspondence between Grantham and Aranda, in 1782, and to a letter from Grantham to Fitzherbert which he was certain would give a similar interpretation. Nevertheless, Fox then reiterated that he could not accept Aranda's interpretation of the preliminary treaty, although he offered no substitute interpretation. He urged Manchester to seek recognition of British rights to remain on the Mosquito Coast, and he further suggested that Manchester explain the situation to Vergennes and request that he try to persuade Aranda to be more accommodating.[41] In a letter of July 6 Manchester reminded Fox that Fox had given him definite directions to agree quickly with Aranda, but even so, Manchester had obtained the extension of the northern boundary to the Hondo River. He assured Fox that he would do all he could to preserve the Mosquito Coast settlements, and he personally doubted that Spain really intended to force the abandonment of all regions outside the defined district.[42] (The attitude of the British ministry and its representatives indicates clearly that they had no comprehension of the policy that Spain had developed in regards to the Caribbean. They were assuming that Spain was proceeding without purpose and endeavoring merely to grasp scattered opportunities to contain English advances.)

Manchester wrote again to Fox on July 9, informing him of the

French opinion which he had sought at Fox's direction. Vergennes had expressed great concern over the impediments encountered and stated that he had understood throughout the negotiations that the Spanish intentions had been to limit all British activities to the defined district. He was certain that Spain could never be persuaded to allow any settlements elsewhere, including those on the Mosquito Coast.[43]

Manchester intimated that the responsibility for this unfortunate commitment on Great Britain's part must be Fitzherbert's or Grantham's, and stressed that had he commenced the negotiations, he would never have consented to the binding article of the preliminary treaty.[44] Although he suggested that the final treaty be signed without this article and the question be settled by a commission within a period of six months after the ratification, he admitted that this was not a very satisfactory method of dealing with the situation.[45] When the proposal was made to Spain, Aranda refused to consider such an option, contending that the issue had to be settled between himself and Manchester.[46]

Thereafter, discussion between Aranda and Manchester achieved little, even though the Englishman sought in every way to obtain a relaxation of the proposed article. Aranda let it be understood that one of Spain's main purposes in the negotiations was to exclude all foreign settlers from any part of the coast from the Gulf of Mexico south to and beyond the Mosquito Coast, and that they would rather continue the war than relax this policy except within that defined district. He admitted that Spain was extremely jealous of any power's —particularly Great Britain's—having any establishments that could encroach upon Spanish colonies in America, especially in areas where local opposition to the Spanish government seemed possible. He noted that this principle applied particularly to the Mosquito Coast and that, therefore, Spain would never grant Britain the right to occupy it. He indicated that he considered Grantham's letter of December 26, 1782 as official acceptance of the projected evacuation and that a disavowal would reflect on the integrity of Great Britain —despite Manchester's insistence that this was a private letter and not a statement of official policy. Manchester then sought French support of his interpretation of the letter as private correspondence without commitment. Gerard de Rayneval, secretary and trusted assistant of Vergennes, upheld the Spanish ambassador and added that the conversation in London bore out his interpretation. In a letter to Fox dated July 24 Manchester held out little hope of further success.[47]

Nevertheless, Manchester persisted in seeking some qualification of the broad commitment to evacuate all other territories. He proposed to Aranda that the word "Spanish" be used to qualify the word "continent." Both Vergennes and Rayneval urged Aranda to accept this minor change, and he did.[48] Manchester then proposed a similar qualification for the word "island," but Aranda did not concur.[49]

Realizing the need for Spanish occupation of the Mosquito Coast, Aranda suggested to the authorities in Madrid that a carefully chosen group should be sent to colonize it. He urged that the expedition be composed of men who could work harmoniously with the contiguous Spanish settlements so that together they could gradually reduce the Indian population and consolidate Spain's control over the area.[50]

The British demand for the right to occupy St. George Island and the right to anchor their ships at the South Triangle Islands was also a recurring issue during the negotiations. As soon as Fox had been informed of the agreement, he had insisted upon recognition of these rights, although the earlier demand for the right to fortify Roatan Island had been dropped. He had written to Manchester that it was of prime importance that the logwood cutters obtain the right to inhabit and use all these islands. Not only were the islands of strategic value, but also the shore of the continent was so infested with flies and generally unwholesome that the settlers could not comfortably live there.[51] There is no evidence that the additional argument was ever used by Manchester. In any event, Aranda refused to grant any right to occupy or fortify the islands, although he reiterated his consent to allow the British to use the islands if they would recognize them as possessions of Spain.[52] As Manchester continued to insist, Aranda reminded the British ambassador that Spain had been very generous in expanding the district from its original offer, thereby granting Great Britain a district of considerable size. He firmly told the ambassador that the British could never get rights over the islands.[53] Still insistent, Manchester pursued the subject with Heredia, who reported their discussions to Aranda.[54] On August 3 Aranda wrote to Manchester informing him respectfully but with finality that he had no authority to change the proposed article as it then read and that Spain would consider no further changes.[55]

Another matter covered by the negotiations was the cutting of mahogany. The preliminary treaty had stated specifically that the district was to be used for cutting logwood. Because the British were deeply interested in obtaining mahogany, Manchester raised the question of their right to cut that wood in the Manatee Lagoon district and elsewhere. Aranda made it clear that they could cut any type of wood they wished within the district but could cut nothing outside of its defined limits.[56]

Negotiations having been concluded, the agreement on Honduras and the rest of Central America was incorporated into Article 6 of the final treaty signed at Versailles by Aranda and Manchester on September 3, 1783. The northern and southern boundaries of the district were set at the Hondo and Belize rivers respectively, with the interior limit defined by certain geographical features at approximately seventy-five miles from the coast. The Hondo and Belize rivers were open to navigation by both nations; and the British were permitted to erect whatever buildings were needed for their living accommodations and their logwood cutting business, but no fortifications. Fishing along the coast was permitted, but not the occupation of the islands. The British had eighteen months to evacuate all other settlements and move into the defined district.[57]

British penetration into Central America had definitely been restricted. The treaty was a successful step in a deliberate Spanish program to develop an effective defense against the British in the Caribbean and the Gulf of Mexico. However, Great Britain had won official recognition of her legal right to occupy a portion of Central America, and was to maintain that foothold until the middle of the twentieth century.

Notes

1. Article 17, Treaty of Paris, 1763, in Gordon Ireland, *Boundaries, Possessions, and Conflicts in Central and North America and the Caribbean* (Boston: Harvard University Press, 1932), p. 122.

2. "Some thoughts relative to the trade lately carried on in the Bay of Honduras and on the Mosquito Shore by the British Merchants," British Museum, Additional Manuscripts, 36806 (hereinafter cited as ADD. MSS.).

3. Vera L. Brown, "Anglo-Spanish Relations in America in the Closing Years of the Colonial Era," *The Hispanic American Historical Review* (August 1922), vol. 5, p. 337.

4. Sir Thomas Robinson, second baron Grantham, secretary of state for colonial affairs, to Alleyne Fitzherbert, minister plenipotentiary, Dec. 12, 1782, British Foreign Office, vol. 27/3; and Fitzherbert to Grantham,

Dec. 18, 1782, British Foreign Office, vol. 27/3 (hereinafter cited as F. O.)

5. Grantham to Fitzherbert, Jan. 9, 1783, F. O., vol. 27/9.

6. Luis Angel Rodríguez, *Carlos III El Rey Catolico que decreto la expulsión de los Jesuitas* (México, D.F.: Editorial Hispano México, 1944), p. 200.

7. These documents cited in Conwell A. Anderson, "Gibraltar: Fortress or Pawn?," *Southwestern Social Science Quarterly* (December 1958), vol. 39, pp. 224-231.

8. Fitzherbert to Grantham, Jan. 19, 1783, F. O., vol. 27/8.

9. "Instrucción para arreglar con la Inglaterra el punto sobre el corte del Palo Campeche, a de Tinte, a consecuencia de lo extipulado por el Art. 4 de los preliminares firmados en Paris el dia 20 de enero de este año, febrero 8, 1783," Archivo Historico Nacional, Madrid, estado legajo 4203, apartado 3 (hereinafter cited as A.H.N.).

10. Grantham to Fitzherbert, Jan. 9, 1783, F. O., vol. 27/9; and Aranda to Floridablanca, Mar. 2, 1783, A.H.N. estado legajo 4223, apartado 1, letter 2392. This river is also referred to in the documents as the Wallis or Bellese; however, Belize appears more frequently and is used in this study.

11. Aranda to Fitzherbert, Mar. 14, 1783, A.H.N., estado legajo 4223, apartado 1, carta 2401.

12. Fitzherbert to Grantham, Mar. 8, 1783, F. O., vol. 27/6.

13. Grantham to Fitzherbert, Mar. 11, 1783, F.O., vol. 27/6.

14. Aranda to Floridablanca, Mar. 2, 1783, A.H.N., estado legajo 4223, apartado 1, carta 2392.

15. Aranda to Floridablanca, Apr. 3, 1783, A.H.N., estado legajo 4223, apartado 1, carta 2414.

16. This river is also referred to in the documents as the Mullino River or the Monas River; however, South Monkey River appears most frequently and is used in this study.

17. "The memorial of His Majesty's Subjects Captivated and Plundered in Yucatan and driven from the Bay of Honduras in September, 1779, on behalf of themselves and the Merchants formerly trading to the said Bay, by Robert White to the Honorable Charles James Fox, His Majesty's Principal Secretary of State for the foreign department, London, June 10, 1783," ADD. MSS., 36806.

18. Ibid.

19. Ibid.

20. Ibid.

21. Ibid.

22. Aranda to Campo, Apr. 13, 1783, A.H.N., estado legajo 4223, apartado 1, letter 2430; and Campo to Fox, Apr. 13, 1783, A.H.N., Estado Legajo 4223, apartado 1, carta 2427.

23. Campo to Aranda, Apr. 20, 1783, A.H.N., estado legajo 4223, apartado 1, carta 2430.

24. Fitzherbert to Fox, May 3, 1783, F. O., vol. 27/8; and Aranda to Campo, May 3, 1783, A.H.N., estado legajo 4223, apartado 1, carta 2444.
25. Fitzherbert to Fox, May 4, 1783, F. O., vol. 27/8.
26. Aranda to Campo, May 3, 1783, A.H.N., estado legajo 4223, apartado 1, carta 2444.
27. Manchester had arrived May 2, 1783. Aranda to Floridablanca, May 3, 1783, A.H.N., estado legajo 4223, apartado 1, carta 2438; and Grantham to Fitzherbert, Apr. 25, 1783, F. O., vol. 27/9.
28. Rayneval to Aranda, May 21, 1783, A.H.N., estado legajo 4233, apartado 1, carta 2444.
29. Aranda to Fox, May 21, A.H.N., estado legajo 4233, apartado 1, carta 2457.
30. See note 16.
31. Manchester to Fox, May 23, 1783, F. O., vol. 27/9; and Fox to Manchester, June 10, 1783, F. O., vol. 27/9.
32. Manchester to Fox, June 18, 1783, F. O., vol. 27/9; Floridablanca to Aranda, June 7, 1783, A.H.N., estado legajo 4233, apartado 2, documento 14; Manchester to Fox, June 18, 1783, F. O., vol. 27/9; and Aranda to Floridablanca, July 12, 1783, A.H.N., estado legajo 4233, apartado 1, carta 2457.
33. "Some thoughts relative to the trade lately carried on in the Bay of Honduras and on the Mosquito Shore by the British Merchants, 1783," ADD. MSS., 36806.
34. John Dalling to Viscount Montstuart, Apr. 17, 1783, ADD. MSS., 36806.
35. Manchester to Fox, June 18, 1783, F. O., vol. 27/9; and Aranda to Floridablanca, July 12, 1783, A.H.N., estado legajo 4233, apartado 1, carta 2457.
36. Manchester to Fox, June 18, 1783, F. O., vol. 27/9.
37. Campo to Aranda, June 28, 1783, A.H.N., estado legajo 4233, apartado 1, carta 2478.
38. See discussion in paragraph three of this article.
39. Manchester to Fox, June 22, 1783, F. O., vol. 27/9.
40. Fox to Manchester, July 2, 1783, F. O., vol. 27/9.
41. Ibid.; Grantham to Fitzherbert, Nov. 28, 1782, quoted in Manchester to Fox, July 6, 1783, F. O., vol. 27/9; Grantham to Aranda, Dec. 26, 1782, quoted in Manchester to Fox, July 6, 1783, F. O., vol. 27/9; and Fitzherbert to Aranda, Feb. 2, 1783, F. O., vol. 27/9.
42. Manchester to Fox, July 6, 1783, F. O., vol. 27/9.
43. Manchester to Fox, July 9, 1783, F. O., vol. 27/9; and George Maddison to William Fraser, July 13, 1783, F. O., vol. 27/6.
44. Manchester to Fox, July 6, 1783, F. O., vol. 27/9.
45. Ibid., July 9, 1783.
46. George Maddison to William Fraser, July 13, 1783, F. O., vol. 27/6.
47. Ibid.; Manchester to Fox, July 13, 1783, F. O., vol. 27/9; Aranda to Floridablanca, July 17, 1783, A.H.N., estado legajo 4233, apartado 1, carta 2482; and Manchester to Fox, July 24, 1783, F. O., vol. 27/9.

48. Aranda to Manchester, July 13, 1783, A.H.N., estado legajo 4233, apartado 1, carta 2482.

49. Manchester to Fox, July 13, 1783, F. O., vol. 27/9.

50. Aranda to Floridablanca, July 17, 1783, A.H.N., estado legajo 4233, apartado 1, carta 2482.

51. Fox to Manchester, July 2, 1783, F. O., vol. 27/9.

52. Aranda to Campo, July 13, 1783, A.H.N., estado legajo 4233, apartado 1, carta 2482.

53. Aranda to Floridablanca, July 17, 1783, A.H.N., estado legajo 4233, apartado 1, carta 2482.

54. Manchester to Fox, Aug. 5, 1783, F. O., vol. 27/6.

55. Aranda to Manchester, Aug. 3, 1783, A.H.N., estado legajo 4233, apartado 1, carta 2495.

56. Aranda to Campo, July 13, 1783, A.H.N., estado legajo 4233, apartado 1, carta 2482; and Manchester to Fox, July 9, 1783, F. O., vol. 27/9.

57. Article 6 of the treaty of peace between Great Britain and Spain was concluded at Versailles, Sept. 3, 1783, and ratified by Spain Sept. 12, 1783. See Charles O. Paullin, ed., *European Treaties Bearing on the History of the United States and Its Dependencies* (Washington: Government Printing Office, 1917–1937), vol. 4, pp. 159–160.

3 | The Religious Impact of the American Occupation of Mexico City, 1847-1848

Edward H. Moseley*

The war between the United States and Mexico was by no means a religious conflict. Political leaders and historians of both nations have agreed that it was primarily a territorial struggle, aggravated by various political and economic factors.[1] It was, however, a war fought between a nation almost totally Roman Catholic and one predominantly Protestant. As the army of Gen. Winfield Scott was pushing up the mountains from Veracruz and entering the Valley of Anahuac, religion had already begun to play a role in the struggle.

As the American army reached the outskirts of Mexico City in August 1847, Gen. Antonio López de Santa Anna issued a stirring proclamation, declaring that God would protect his people and chastise the invading heretics.[2] Many citizens flocked in panic to the cathedral to hear a solemn mass and to ask for divine assistance in the defense of their city against the "Yankee devils." [3]

When the Mexican army abandoned the capital, many natives considered the American occupation to be "nothing less than the chastisement of Heaven."[4] One disheartened soldier lamented: "His Divine Majesty has sent these devils to punish us for our sins." [5] Others were more optimistic and continued to express a hope that God would eventually liberate them from the foreign oppressor.[6]

In the United States also, many religious leaders saw a relationship between divine will and the success of American arms. In the southern states especially, preachers stood behind President James K. Polk, accepted the doctrine of Manifest Destiny and saw the ultimate triumph of Protestantism as one of the justifications for the war.[7]

* The author wishes to thank the American Philosophical Society for a grant that made it possible for him to do research in Mexico City, and find the basic materials used in this paper.

The editor of the *Tennessee Baptist* expressed a hope that an American victory would ". . . open Mexico to the preaching of the Gospel." [8] Upon hearing of the capture of Mexico City, the Presbyterian Synod of Mississippi declared that the doors of the conquered nation had been ". . . opened by the Providence of God," and that denomination, therefore, took steps to extend its missionary activities into those parts of Mexico that had been occupied by the United States.[9] Politicians, too, attributed the success of American arms to divine intervention. John Y. Mason, secretary of the navy, declared the conquest to be "one of the greatest events of civilization and Christianity." [10] Southerners especially, emphasized the justice of the struggle and denounced as fanatical abolitionists all who opposed it.[11]

At the scene of victory the triumphant forces saw divine guidance as partly responsible for their success. On Sunday, October 3, 1847 the Reverend Mr. McCarty, chaplain of the American army, delivered a special thanksgiving sermon. He assured his audience that the war had been "necessary and right," and for that reason ". . . the great Disposer of events, who holds the very winds in his fist," had guided the American armies to victory.[12] But, triumph, according to the chaplain, brought responsibility. He admonished the soldiers:

> Let us realize that He has not preserved and brought us here to 'revel in the Halls of Montezuma,' but to serve Him and do our duty; especially by turning our success and our consequent influence over this people into the means of enlightening their religious ignorance and raising them from the degradation to which they are reduced. And this by extending the light and the blessings of our purer faith; so that by our Christian influence and example and by the intercourse between us, they may imbibe something of our free spirit and throw off the shackles of military and spiritual despotism.[13]

He warned, however, that the purer faith of Protestantism could triumph only if the soldiers would keep themselves free from the ". . . vices to which military men are most tempted and addicted. . . ." [14] This was indeed a challenge to a victorious army in a strange and exotic land.

Enterprising American businessmen and women rushed into Mexico to provide goods and services that were designed to test the faith and morals of the Protestant victors. Establishments with such nostalgic names as the St. Louis House, the Old Kentucky Restaurant, and the Lone Star House rivalled each other in an attempt to quench the thirst of the soldiers. The proprietors of the Eagle Coffee House boasted of services "on the American style," where no expense was spared to provide customers with "Wines, Liquors and Segars of the choisest brand." [15] On Christmas Day of 1847 Mrs. Sarah Foyle, manager of the Theatre Coffee House, announced that, ". . . having received a small quantity of pure Monongahela Whiskey, she [was] prepared to furnish her customers with hot Whiskey Punches, Tom and Jerry, Egg Nogs, &c." [16] In addition to these sophisticated establishments, scores of local bars and *pulquerias* offered wares that were less familiar but just as effective. Americans were surprised to see *cantinas* with such names as "Jésus y María" or "El Amor de Diós," but they patronized them with little hesitation. [17]

Records of courts-martial reveal many cases of drunkenness and disorderly conduct among the occupation forces. [18] Lt. John S. Devlin of the United States Marine Corps seems to have exceeded all others in his antics. In 1847 Devlin was drunk on duty September 9, 10, 12 and 19. Then, on September 22 he ". . . was so drunk at the quarters of the Marine Regiment . . . as to disturb, by his noise, the officers of the Regiment until a late hour of the night." Furthermore, he

> . . . did while in a state of intoxication, at or near the village of San Angel, dress himself in an unofficerlike and ridiculous manner, and ride at full speed, on horseback, through the streets, to the amusement of the privates and the mortification of the officers of the regiment to which he belong[ed.] [19]

Finally, after being drunk on two other occasions and threatening his commanding officer, young Devlin was court-martialed and discharged from the service. [20]

General Scott expressed grave concern over the excessive drinking, and general breakdown of discipline. [21] One group of soldiers, concerned over the extent of the problem, organized a chapter of the Brothers of Temperance, and expressed the hope that by their example they might ". . . crush the Hydra-headed Monster, Intemperance!, the bane of society, the foundation of wrong, the progenitor of crime, dissensions, and vices." [22] As might be expected, efforts to curb drinking fell far short of complete success, and the image of the Protestant religion suffered in the eyes of the Catholic natives. José Fernando Ramírez commented in September of 1847:

> I have never before seen such sodden drunkenness, nor any more scandalous or impudent than the drunkenness that holds these men in

its grip. Nor have I ever seen more unrestrained appetites. Every hour of the day, except during the evenings, when they are all drunk, one can find them eating everything they see.[23]

American soldiers found diversions other than those of the bottle. Bull fights, theaters, gambling houses, and cock fights offered thrills and excitement.[24] Many soldiers who went to the racetracks placed bets on the favorite of the 1847 season, a pacer named James K. Polk.[25] A circus promised homesick Yankees a variety of amazing and rare spectacles. The editor of the *Daily American Star* warned of the moral pitfalls that awaited the spectator. "Madame Turin," he stated, "is a fearless and daring rider, but by no manner of means as chaste as we would be pleased to see her . . . for her present dress is indecent for the service, to say the least of it." [26] This condemnation may not be entirely unrelated to another comment made in the same issue: "There was an unusually large attendance at the Circus night before last. . . ." [27]

Of all the attractions that confronted the men of the occupation force, none carried more temptation or potential danger than women. Mexican men naturally resented the attempts by American soldiers to gain the favor of the local women.[28] It became quite common in the city, however, to see Americans with Mexican ladies by their sides, and many señoritas became "Yankeefied" as they began to wear shawls and bonnets in place of their traditional rebozos.[29] Success with the ladies boosted the ego of some troopers to a point of excessive vanity. One Texan exclaimed, "*Mexicanas*, like all other women, love to associate with the truly valiant of the lords of creation, and where can Texas be beat for her bravery." [30] Certain "ladies," however, were persuaded by more material offerings, and the number of professional prostitutes in the city grew to meet the increased demand.[31]

Love affairs added to the already tense atmosphere of the Mexican capital. Numerous fights and squabbles broke out in dance halls, grogshops, and other public places. In October 1847, a South Carolina volunteer stabbed a member of his regiment at the New Orleans Coffee House, killing him instantly.[32] Several weeks later a group of New Yorkers in the Progreso Bar attacked two sergeants of the Ninth Infantry, causing their hospitalization.[33] Fraternal squabbles were frequent among the occupation forces, but most of the acts of violence involved Americans and members of the local community.

These clashes often resulted in serious injuries or death to the participants.[34]

It would be unfair to brand all the Americans who occupied Mexico City as drunkards, brawlers, or moral degenerates. The individuals whose escapades reached the official files were certainly in the minority. Some Mexican spokesmen admitted that the conduct of the invasion force was better than they had expected.[35] Nevertheless, American soldiers did not serve as perfect examples of the "purer form of religion" that Chaplain McCarty had placed before them as a goal. Mexican observers, who already held hostile opinions of the invader, naturally recorded and remembered the actions of the disorderly and criminal *norteamericanos*. The memory of the drunken and depraved Protestant persists in Mexican legends and in history books, while the sober and upright actions of the majority of the invaders have long since passed from memory.[36] General Scott lamented the fact that the excesses of a small number of individuals brought disgrace not only to the army, but also to the entire United States.[37]

It would be difficult to avoid the conclusion that the American occupation of Mexico City did very little to convert its natives to the Protestant faith. This failure was not due to any unusual characteristics or actions on the part of the American soldiers. Medieval crusaders, and even the Children of Israel, had failed to set a perfect example of morality and faith among conquered peoples. What could one expect of the Protestant frontiersmen who had seized sophisticated, metropolitan Mexico City? In the long run, however, the occupation did produce some significant religious results. These were related to domestic politics and to the official policies carried out by the American officials during the occupation.

Even if all the American soldiers in the Mexican capital had set perfect examples of moral and spiritual conduct, it is unlikely that they would have produced a victory for Protestantism. Gen. Winfield Scott subordinated the religious question in Mexico to military and political objectives. In the light of these objectives, the spread of the Protestant faith was not to the advantage of the American cause. Wishing to discredit all rumors and fears, the general issued a series of proclamations in which he assured the people of Mexico that the Americans had no intention of disrupting their religious system.[38] Not only did he strictly forbid the "wanton desecration of churches, cemeteries, or other religious edifices," but he also urged the troops to show respect for Catholic services.[39] When Irish Catholics deserted the American cause, the commander attempted to discount any religious implications of that incident.[40]

Soon after the surrender of Mexico City, General Scott made a personal effort to gain the confidence of the Mexican clergy. He ordered the reopening of all churches, personally attended services at the cathedral, and issued a statement in which he asserted, ". . . nothing is better calculated to produce harmony between us [and the Mexican people] than the worship of the God we all reverence at the same altar." [41]

The efforts of the American commander were largely successful. High church dignitaries received him with great courtesy during a visit to the Shrine of Guadalupe in early October 1847.[42] Archbishop Juan Manuel Irizarri y Peralta expressed his personal pleasure at the respect shown by American officials for the Mexican Church.[43] When the archbishop visited General Scott in early November to make arrangements for the release of Mexican prisoners, rumors circulated throughout the city that the American commander had accepted Catholicism and was receiving baptism.[44] This rumor was false, but it illustrates the cordial relationship which existed between the two men.[45]

General Scott considered his relationship with Mexican ecclesiastical leaders to be in accordance with American ideals of liberalism, tolerance, and freedom of religion.[46] In the light of Mexican conditions, however, his policies took on a very different meaning. The Catholic Church claimed an exclusive position in the field of religion, and the American commander's cooperation with that institution could hardly be considered as an effort to promote religious tolerance or "liberalism." But in the long run the American occupation and General Scott's relationship with the Mexican Church *did* help to bring about a major religious change in Mexico. This change was related to the complex relationship between Church and State there which had its foundations in the colonial period.

The Catholic Church was a very important force in the conquest of New Spain, acquiring extensive property holdings in the process. Upon establishing its independence, Mexico recognized Catholicism as the only religion of the nation and guaranteed its properties and special privileges, or *fueros*. By 1824, the Church controlled about one-fourth of the entire wealth of Mexico. Furthermore, it enjoyed the status of a tax-exempt and virtually sovereign corporation.[47]

From the very beginning of the national period, liberal thinkers and politicians denounced the Church as an institution opposed to the best interests of the State. José María Luis Mora advocated freeing Mexican society from clerical shackles and feudalism.[48] In 1833 Valentín Gómez Farías, leader of the liberal forces, attempted to reduce the *fueros* of the clergy and take over part of the ecclesiastical wealth for the support of the bankrupt state.[49] The general population of Mexico refused to support a program that called for such a radical break with established institutions and traditions.

When the United States declared war on Mexico, government officials realized that vast resources would be needed to defend the nation. Since the Church possessed the only sizable amount of movable wealth in the nation, it was only natural for political leaders to turn to that quarter for financial support. Gómez Farías, having been returned to power by the maneuvering of Santa Anna, took steps once again to extract some of the clerical wealth, this time for national defense. Archbishop Irizarri denounced his demands, asserting that the Church was immune from any taxation by the secular government. Because Gómez Farías pressed the issue, the Church supported a military rebellion. This resulted in the overthrow of the government and prepared the way for the return of Santa Anna to the center of the political arena.[50]

Differences between Church and State were settled for outward appearances, and the clergy even agreed to make "voluntary contributions" for the defense of the nation.[51] Many Mexican officials, however, denounced these efforts as insufficient and blamed the Church for the collapse of the defenses of the capital. José Fernando Ramírez was bitter in his attack; he reported to a friend: "Several prominent dignitaries of the church have stated that if the Yankees respect their religion and their property, they can lose nothing through invasion." [52] As the United States army moved against the city, the Mexican clergy contributed prayers but no material support.[53] It is in the light of these conditions that the American occupation and the policies of General Scott should be considered.

In the name of liberalism and religious freedom, the American commander assured the Mexican Church that it would be protected in the exercise of its worship and in its property.[54] Mexican Liberals interpreted this to mean that the American general, in exchange for the cooperation of the clergy, was leaving the vast wealth and special privileges of the Mexican Church undisturbed. At the same time, the Mexican nation was being forced to surrender one-third of its territory as a result of the humiliating defeat at the hands of the Protestant foe. As the army of the United States withdrew, many Liberals blamed the Mexican Church for their plight, and denounced it for treason against the State.[55]

In the decade following the Treaty of Guadalupe Hidalgo, Mexico experienced economic depression and social anarchy. In 1858 a vicious civil war erupted, the War of Reform. Political and economic factors were probably more important causes of this conflict than religion. The Liberals, however, struck at the *fueros* and riches of the Church, proclaiming that it was contrary to the best interests of the nation for them to remain in the hands of the clergy. Naturally the Church opposed these efforts and denounced them as antireligious. Thus the war took on the name *Reforma*, reminiscent of the great European upheaval of the sixteenth century. It is beyond the scope of this paper to record the far-reaching influences of the War of Reform, but it might be noted that it has come to be recognized as one of the central events in the evolution of the Mexican nation.[56]

Mexican liberals who participated in the *Reforma* traced its ideology to the Enlightenment and to nineteenth-century European liberalism. Historically they considered it to be a revival of the movement begun by Padre Miguel Hidalgo y Costilla in 1810.[57] In addition, however, the occupation of Mexico by the forces of the United States helped to produce both the ideals and historical events of this important movement.

Practically all the leaders of the War of the Reform, including Benito Juárez, witnessed the events of 1847–1848. They blamed the archaic organization of the Mexican nation, and singled out the Church as the guilty party in its perpetuation. Furthermore, the failure of the clergy to provide needed funds to defend the nation, and the actual cooperation with the foreign commander on the part of the archbishop helped to convince these leaders that basic changes in Church-State relationships were necessary.[58] The Yankee occupation influenced the Reform movement in other ways also. During the time United States forces were in Mexico there was a free exchange of ideas, including liberal concepts in economics. Schemes to build railroads, canals, and other facilities were popular, and were propagandized in the English-language newspapers.[59] Many of the same ideas were popular with the leaders of the Reform movement ten years later.[60]

Finally, the period of American occupation was one in which religious ideals and moral values were openly discussed. Bibles were introduced by the Protestant invaders and were often made available to curious Mexicans. It is even possible that the loose conduct of the American soldiers did not completely nullify their "Protestant virtues." Following the triumph of the Liberal forces in the War of the Reform, President Juárez ordered the removal of all obscene and indecent pictures from the walls of the *pulquerias* of Mexico City.[61] This decree would certainly have gained the approval of persons who had dreamed of the establishment of a "purer faith" in Mexico.

It is obvious that Protestantism did not flourish in Mexico following the withdrawal of the army of the United States in 1848. With the success of the Reform movement, however, and with the advance of liberal concepts, Mexico did achieve a new degree of religious freedom.[62] Concepts of tolerance, common both to the Protestant invaders and the Liberals, eventually led to the return of Protestant missionaries. They came back, not by military conquest, but by invitation.[63]

Notes

1. Justin H. Smith, *The War With Mexico*, 2 vols. (New York: The Macmillan Company, 1919), vol. 1, pp. 72, 83, 102–103, 117, 125; George Lockhart Rives, *The United States and Mexico, 1821–1848*, 2 vols. (New York: Charles Scribner's Sons, 1913), vol. 2, pp. 22–80; Otis A. Singletary, *The Mexican War* (Chicago: University of Chicago Press, 1960), pp. 1–5, 14–27; Emilio Rabasa, *La Evolución Historica de México* (México, D.F.: Editorial Porrua, S.A. 1956), p. 42; *El Siglo Diez y Nueve*, Jan. 23, 1863; and U.S. *Executive Documents*, No. 60, 13th Congress, 1st sess., *Messages of the President of the United States, with the correspondence, therewith communicated, between the Secretary of War and Other Officers of the Government, on the Subject of: The Mexican War*, James K. Polk, "Hostilities by Mexico: Message from the President of the United States relative to an invasion and commencement of hostilities by Mexico," May 11, 1846 (Washington, D.C.: Wendell and Van Benthuysen, Printers, 1848) (hereinafter cited as *Messages of the President*).

2. "Proclamation of Santa Anna," Aug. 9, 1847, *Daily American Star*, Nov. 24, 1847. This newspaper began publication soon after the American occupation of Mexico City (Sept. 20, 1847) under the title of *American Star*, and then changed the title to *Daily American Star* after Oct. 12,

1847. It contained an English-language section and a Spanish-language section.

3. Juan G. to My Dear Jesusita, Aug. 21, 1847, *Daily American Star*, Oct. 16, 1847. "The temples were full of Mexicans, praying to God for a triumph of our arms." See also Guillermo Prieto, *Memorias de Mis Tiempos, 1828 a 1853*, 2 vols. (Paris and México: Libreria de la Vda. de C. Bouret, 1906), vol. 2, p. 208; and José María Roa Barcena, *Recuerdos de la Invasion Norteamericana: 1846–1848*, 3 vols. (México: Colección de Escritores Mexicanos, Editorial Porrua, S.A., 1947), vol. 2, p. 178.

4. Juan G. to My Dear Jesusista, Aug. 21, 1847, *Daily American Star*, Oct. 16, 1847.

5. J.M.G. to My Dear Mother, Aug. 21, 1847, *Daily American Star*, Oct. 15, 1847.

6. C. to My Never-Forgotten and Beloved Catila, Aug. 21, 1847, *Daily American Star*, Oct. 17, 1847.

7. *Tennessee Baptist*, June 5, 1847; Oct. 16, 1847; Dec. 18, 1847; *Alabama Baptist*, Jan. 8, 1847; and *Southwestern Baptist Chronicle* (New Orleans, La.), June 19, 1847; Oct. 9, 1847; Oct. 23, 1847; Nov. 6, 1847; Dec. 18, 1847. In the Oct. 23, 1847 issue the editor stated: "We are believers in the superintendence of a directing Providence . . . impressed with a conviction, that the decree is made, and in the process execution, that this continent is to be but one nation. . . ."

8. *Tennessee Baptist*, June 19, 1847. "Wonder what sort of a God theirs can be! He is not the Christian God, certainly. Thus, too, the Roman Catholics in Mexico are to lose their holy sacraments . . . The religion of China is as fully christian, and just as good as this. God grant that the war now in progress, may be so [concluded] as to open Mexico to the preaching of the Gospel."

9. "Minutes from the Synod of Mississippi," n.d. *Daily American Star*, Jan. 25, 1848.

10. *Daily American Star*, Dec. 18, 1847.

11. "Address by Aaron B. Brown to the Senate and House of Representatives of the State of Tennessee," October, 1847, *Tennessee Baptist*, Oct. 16, 1847.

12. "A Thanksgiving Sermon," *Daily American Star*, Oct. 24, 1847.

13. Ibid.

14. Ibid.

15. *Daily American Star*, Oct. 28, 1847.

16. *Daily American Star*, Jan. 1, 1848. "P.S. She would be happy to see her old Texan friends at any time."

17. *Daily American Star*, Dec. 11, 1847.

18. *Daily American Star*, Nov. 12, 1847; Sept. 23, 1847; and Dec. 19, 1847.

19. *Daily American Star*, Nov. 14, 1847.

20. Ibid.

21. *Messages of the President*, Winfield Scott to the Secretary of War, Dec. 25, 1847, pp. 1047–1049.

22. "Brothers of Temperance," *Daily American Star*, Nov. 21, 1847.

23. José Fernando Ramírez to Don Francisco Elorriaga, Sept. 30, 1847, in José Fernando Ramírez, *México During the War with the United States*, trans. Elliott B. Scherr, and ed. Walter V. Scholes (Columbia, Mo.: University of Missouri Press, 1950), pp. 160–162.

24. *Daily American Star*, Jan. 7, 1848. Three gaming houses were licensed by authorities of the United States.

25. *Daily American Star*, Nov. 16, 1847.

26. "Madame Turin," *Daily American Star*, Oct. 16, 1847.

27. *Daily American Star*, Oct. 16, 1847.

28. M.M.Z. to Guillermo Prieto, n.d., in Prieto, *Memorias*, vol. 2, pp. 254–255; and *American Star*, Sept. 30, 1847.

29. *Daily American Star*, Nov. 30, 1847.

30. "The Texan Ball," *Daily American Star*, Dec. 8, 1847. The author expressed a willingness to bet that there would be ". . . more pretty women there than has graced any ballroom since our arrival in this city. . . ."

31. M.M.Z. to Guillermo Prieto, in Prieto, *Memorias*, vol. 2, pp. 254–255. "Allí lucían, como no es posible explicar, *las Margaritas*, así bautizadas por los *yankees* las mujeres perdidas, que se multiplicaron extraordinariamente, porque sus favorecedores regaban para ellas el dinero."; and Roa Barcena, *Recuerdos*, vol. 3, p. 200. ". . . había cantinas, mesas de juego, bailes y orgías, y templos destinados al culto de la Venus más callejera y desarrapada."

32. "Stabbing," *Daily American Star*, Oct. 28, 1847.

33. *Daily American Star*, Dec. 5, 1847.

34. *Daily American Star*, Nov. 2, 1847; Nov. 9, 1847; Dec. 19, 1847; Jan. 11, 1848; Jan. 29, 1848. In the Nov. 9, 1847 issue the editor stated: "We understand that there was one or two considerable rows on Sunday last, between Americans and Mexicans, and that several deaths ensued."

35. Ramírez, *México*, pp. 160–162. "I must say that those who have conquered us, brutally savage as they are, have conducted themselves in a manner different from that of European armies belonging to the nations that bear the standard of civilization. This does not mean that they do not commit countless excesses. . . . But we have here a phenomenon consisting of mingled barbarism and restraint." See also "Statement by the Ayuntamiento of Toluca," *Daily American Star*, Jan. 14, 1848.

36. M.M.Z. to Guillermo Prieto, n.d., in Prieto, *Memorias*, vol. 2, pp. 254–255; Tu N. to Guillermo Prieto, n.d., Prieto, *Memorias*, vol. 2, pp. 248–251; *Liberal Verdadero*, Jan. 13, 1848, quoted in *Daily American Star*, Jan. 29, 1848; "To My Dear friend," Sept. 30, 1847, in Ramírez, *México*, pp. 160–162; and Roa Barcena, *Recuerdos*, vol. 3, p. 200.

37. *Messages of the President*, Winfield Scott to Secretary of War, Dec. 25, 1847, pp. 1047–1049. "I do not mean to accuse the reinforcements, generally, of deficiency in valor, patriotism, or moral character, Far from it; but among all new levies, of whatever denomination, there are always a few miscreants in every hundred, enough, without *discipline*, to disgrace the entire mass, and what is infinitely worse—the *country* that employs them."

38. *Messages of the President*, "Proclamation: To the good people of

Mexico," Apr. 11, 1847, p. 937; and *Messages of the President*, "Proclamation to the Mexican People," May 11, 1847, pp. 968–971.

39. *American Star*, Sept. 20, 1847; Sept. 25, 1847; and General Orders No. 297, Headquarters of the Army, Mexico, Sept. 24, 1847, *American Star*, Sept. 25, 1847. ". . . either keep out of the way, or to pay to the catholic religion and its ceremonies every decent mark of respect and deference."

40. General Order No. 296, Sept. 22, 1847, *American Star*, Sept. 23, 1847. In this order General Scott praised the loyal Catholics of the American army and denounced the bribery which had been used to lure some to the Mexican side.

41. *American Star*, Sept. 23, 1847.

42. *American Star*, Oct. 12, 1847.

43. *Messages of the President*, Juan Manuel, archbishop of Cesarea, to Winfield Scott, Nov. 5, 1847, pp. 1054–1055.

44. *Daily American Star*, Nov. 6, 1847. ". . . y algunos espresaron su creencia de que el general se iba volver *cristiano*, y que su santidad lo fué a bautizar."

45. *Messages of the President*, Winfield Scott to archbishop of Mexico, Dec. 21, 1847, p. 1057; *Messages of the President*, Juan Manuel to Winfield Scott, Dec. 23, 1847, p. 1057; and *Messages of the President*, "Address by the Archbishop of Mexico to Mexican Soldiers," pp. 1058–1059. These documents further illustrate the close relationship between the archbishop and General Scott.

46. *American Star*, Sept. 25, 1847. "General Scott himself, we know to be a strong Protestant, but he is liberal enough and gentlemanly enough to respect the ceremonies of other denominations." See also, General Orders No. 297, Headquarters of the Army, Mexico, Sept. 24, 1847, *American Star*, Sept. 25, 1847.

47. John Lloyd Mecham, *Church and State in Latin America: A History of Politico-Ecclesiastical Relations* (Chapel Hill: University of North Carolina Press, 1934), pp. 395–402. The Constitution of 1824 provided: " 'The nation will protect [the Catholic Church] by wise and just laws and prohibits the exercise of any other.' " Mecham comments: "Independence . . . only served to aggrandize the Church in wealth and prestige."

48. Daniel Moreno, *Los hombres de la Reforma* (México, D.F.: Ediciones Libro-Mex., 1956), p. 16. In this work the author quotes Mora: " 'Cada mexicano debe preguntarse diariamente a sí mismo si el pueblo existe para el clero o si el clero ha sido creado para satisfacer las necesidades del pueblo.' "

49. Mecham, *Church and State*, pp. 404–412. The author demonstrates that there has been a wide variety of interpretations as to the motives and aims of these movements. One factor is clear, however, they intended to attack the property and *fueros* of the Church, and they did so in the name of the State. He says: "The opening gun of the Liberal attack was aimed at the ecclesiastical temporalities. The opulence of the Church contrasted with the empty public treasury."

50. Roa Barcena, *Recuerdos,* vol. 2, p. 171; and José Fernando Ramírez to Elorriaga, June 5, 1847, in Ramírez, *México,* p. 123.

52. Ramírez to Elorriaga, Apr. 25, 1847, in Ramírez, *México,* p. 123; Moreno, *Los hombres de la Reforma,* p. 8; and Ralph Roeder, *Juarez and his Mexico,* 2 vols. (New York: The Viking Press, 1947), vol. 1, p. 69. Roeder stated: ". . . the credit of a corporation that acknowledged no civil obligations sank in public respect past recovery."

53. Prieto, *Memorias,* vol. 2, pp. 201–203. He had visited Archbishop Irizarri, requesting support for the city's defense, but the archbishop denied the right of the State to make the demand and refused to make any contribution.

54. *Messages of the President,* "Proclamation to the Mexican People," May 11, 1847, pp. 968–971. "Los bienes de la iglesia amenazados y presentados como aliciente para la revolución y la anarquía; la fortuna de los ricos propietarios señalada para rapiña de los perversos." He promised the protection of property against lawless action.

55. Prieto, *Memorias,* vol. 2, pp. 201–203, 211. He stated that as the Americans pushed against the city persons of all parties helped in the defense, except some foreigners *and* the members of the clergy.

56. Walter V. Scholes, *Mexican Politics During the Juárez Regime 1855–1872* (Columbia, Mo.: The University of Missouri Studies, 1957), pp. 1–6; Mecham, *Church and State,* pp. 427–429; and Charles A. Hale, *Mexican Liberalism in the Age of Mora, 1821–1853* (New Haven and London: Yale University Press, 1968), pp. 39–147.

57. *El Siglo Diez y Nueve,* Aug. 21, 1861; "La Reforma," *La Opinion Liberal,* quoted in *El Siglo Diez y Nueve,* Sept. 6, 1861; and *El Siglo Diez y Nueve,* Jan. 27, 1863. In this last issue the famous liberal editor Francisco Zarco declares a relationship with the French Revolution, but considers the Mexican *Reforma* to have gone further for religious freedom. "Proclamando la libertad absoluta de la conciencia . . . a la independencia absoluta de la religion del yugo del Estado."; see also *El Siglo Diez y Nueve,* Mar. 29, 1863.

58. Moreno, *Los hombres,* pp. 8, 12. He points out that those who drew up the Constitution of 1857 were in large part those who had witnessed the days of the American invasion; and Roeder, *Juarez and his Mexico,* vol. 1, pp. 66–69. Roeder expresses the opinion that the war against the United States played an important part in the career of Benito Juárez, the man who was to become the personification of the *Reforma.*

59. *Daily American Star,* Oct. 7, 1847; "Isthmus of Tehuantepec," *Daily American Star,* Nov. 20, 1847; "The Railroad," *Daily American Star,* Dec. 3, 1847; and "Railroad from Vera Cruz to Mexico. Preliminary Meeting," *Daily American Star,* Dec. 5, 1847.

60. *El Siglo Diez y Nueve,* Jan. 21, 1861; Jan. 26, 1861; and Jan. 1, 1863.

61. "Pulquerias," *El Siglo Diez y Nueve,* June 14, 1862; El Estado y El Clero en México," *El Siglo Diez y Nueve,* Sept. 6, 1861; "El Cristianismo y la Democracia," *El Siglo Diez y Nueve,* Oct. 9, 1861; and "Fanatismo," *El Siglo Diez y Nueve,* Oct. 19, 1862. The articles listed above show in-

teresting relationships between ideas of the Mexican Liberals and the American Protestants.

62. "El Clero y la Nación," *El Siglo Diez y Nueve*, Aug. 21, 1861; and "El Cristianismo y la Democracia," *El Siglo Diez y Nueve*, Oct. 9, 1861. It should be noted that the success of the Liberals in the War of the Reform did not end the struggle concerning the position of the Church in Mexico. This problem has persisted into the twentieth century.

63. Mecham, *Church and State*, pp. 453–455.

4 | The Forty-Niners in Panama: Canal Prelude

Eugene R. Huck

By the middle of the nineteenth century a tremendous struggle was underway between Great Britain and the United States for expansion into Latin America. The United States was generally interested in acquiring land, and in particular land adjoining its southern border. Its people were intoxicated with the idea of Manifest Destiny; and James K. Polk, an expansionist president, was engaged in schemes to extend United States boundaries both in the Oregon territory and in the Southwest. The United States became involved in Central America not only through the filibusterer William C. Walker,[1] but also through official emissaries such as Elijah Hise, Ephraim G. Squier, and Benjamin A. Bidlack—all of whom were attempting to get Isthmian concessions from at least three different Central American countries.

Great Britain on its part was generally interested in selling the products of its industrial revolution and specifically in using Isthmian communication to this end. The agitation on the Mosquito Coast and in Nicaragua tended to confirm suspicions in Washington that Great Britain had territorial designs that included California.[2] At the outbreak of the Mexican War the United States took possession of San Francisco Bay[3] and countered British advances in Panama by the negotiation of a treaty with New Granada.

Benjamin A. Bidlack, the United States minister to New Granada, was fully aware of the importance of the Isthmus of Panama in the future plans of the United States. Although he possessed no instructions on the subject, his eagerness to capitalize on an enigmatic offer of transit rights across Panama caused him to negotiate a treaty of amity and commerce late in 1846, which gave preferential Isthmian consideration to the United States.[4] It took exactly a year and a half to get the treaty approved, but when it was ratified it opened new opportunities for expansion to the south.[5]

The happy accident of the discovery of gold in California came on the heels of the treaty. The basic provision assured the right of transit across the province of Panama by any means in return for the guarantee of the national sovereignty of New Granada over the area. This meant that, in theory, the Forty-Niners were to receive the same considerations and concessions in their passage as did the nationals. In practice, however, some problems existed. *Latinos* were all too familiar with the ways of United States filibusterers and soldiers but knew little of the peacetime *Yanqui*. They learned a great deal during the rapid influx of *norteamericanos* into Panama in 1849 and afterwards.

The *Yanqui* gold-hunter en route to California by way of Panama was probably tormented by boredom during his journey. It is likely that he spent much of his time from New York or New Orleans to the Isthmus examining his new flannel shirt or heavy boots or simply dreaming of his future wealth. One may rest assured, however, that he had selected the route through Panama because he was told by the shipping agents that it would take "only weeks" as opposed to months around Cape Horn or overland by wagon. Government oceanic mail service had been started in 1849 from New York to the Isthmus and from the western coast of Panama to San Francisco. This indicated that the United States government thought highly of the route.[6] Although the trip was expensive (average cost: $380), hopes were high that the investment would be richly repaid when the traveler reached California. With these thoughts in mind, the adventurer debarked at Chagres, unaware of the uncomfortable passage ahead and a possible delay of weeks—with more expense while waiting for a ship to California.[7]

The standard way of getting from Chagres on the Caribbean to Panama City on the Pacific was uncomfortable, if not torturous. A traveler could contract for passage on a small shallow-draught steamer up the Chagres River to the town of Gorgona, about twenty-five miles inland. From there, he could expect two days of travel by mule train across the mountains of Panama to the Pacific. If the passenger arrived during the wet season, the trip to Gorgona took about two days. But if he were unfortunate enough to arrive in the dry season, his steamer would become stranded in the Chagres after only about ten or twelve miles, and he would have to go the rest of the way by canoe.[8]

A certain Mr. Turner, however, apparently had special contacts or good fortune, because on March 29, 1850 he was able to make the trip, which usually took four days even in the wet season, in twenty-eight hours. A newspaper account of this fact does not say whether this was road time or total time, but it does say that it was the shortest time ever achieved. However, the paper notes, it was Mr. Turner's "usual practice" to travel with "telegraphic speed." [9]

As the flow of people increased in 1850, improvements of the Isthmian passage were expected. In July 1850, a Mississippi riverboat captain proposed to construct a boat capable of making the run from Chagres to Gorgona regardless of the depth of the Chagres River. The *Star*, a newspaper published in Panama City, commented: "the successful experiment of constructing a boat suitable for the navigation of the Chagres River is looked upon by many as unpractical." [10] The reason given was not that the obstacles in the river were vexatious, but that a boat to be capable of making the run would have to have a draught of less than eighteen inches. Various individuals and companies, such as the Panama Railway Company, had boats especially constructed by the Chelsea Iron Works of New York City,[11] but in point of fact there was no significant improvement of the Isthmian passage until completion of the railroad in 1855.

The Cincinnati *Gazette* of March 23, 1850, as quoted in the *Star*, stated that a gentleman had left that city with three hundred mules and seven barges to form a communication system across the Isthmus of Panama. He informed the reporter that they would

> be placed at "easy stages" along the route to Panama for packing merchandise . . . [and that he had a plan] also in view for conveying meats, and poultry, etc. over the Isthmus in packages which [had] a surface of a charcoal composition on them to preserve them pure and sweet.[12]

Thus plans for transportation included supplies as well as human beings, and enterprising businessmen far from the Isthmus intended to capitalize on the travel-mania.

The first contact between the *Yanqui* and *Latino* cultures, then, related to the transportation of United States citizens and goods across the Isthmus to the city of Panama. As might be expected, problems developed from this contact. On June 19, 1850, for example, a Panamanian stole a coat from a *Yanqui* transient. The thief abandoned the canoe in which he was transporting the traveler and swam to the side of the river where most of his fellow citizens lived. He was pursued by a group of *Yanquis,* who were fired upon from a "castle" (probably a fortified wooden structure), which was stormed and captured.[13]

The *Star* referred to the antagonists as "natives" on one side of the river and "Americans" on the other. The local Spanish-language paper, *El Panameño,* issued a stinging editorial in its next edition, saying that it had tried to be friendly and to include in its columns articles coming from the United States that would be of interest to all readers. The editor, however, apparently felt that the Yankees were not only causing trouble, but were also claiming land that was not rightfully theirs. In one issue it was stated:

> We wish that the provincial government might take official warning, to the end that it is not going to strip us little by little of our sovereignty over our own territory and that those that come to populate it will not fail to submit to our constitution and laws.[14]

Other news items and editorials in the *Star* reflected attitudes of the travelers from the United States regarding the Panamanian residents. In citing a Chagres fire in mid-March 1850, which burned some twenty-five bamboo huts, not only did the *Star* refer to it as being confined to the "native" side; it also noted that a number of game chickens were presumed to be lost and that it was not known whether the huts were insured. No mention was made of possible loss of "native" life. The *Yanquis,* it seemed, valued only the game chickens, as objects of sport, and had the náiveté to question whether the hut-inhabiting natives had any fire insurance.[15]

It is not surprising that crime existed in nineteenth-century Panama. Cases were reported of murders and robberies among United States citizens or among the local citizens, but they can be dismissed as being within a single cultural framework. Intercultural riots and fights seemed legion, and both sides suffered casualties. In a June 7, 1850 article, under the lead of "Lynch Law," the editor of the *Star* readily admitted that harsh treatment of Panamanians by United States citizens had caused the recent riot. He said:

> . . . natives have been abused, beat and pounded and have generally received shameful treatment at the hands of the bad and vicious of our countrymen [for more than a year] and have at last become so excitable that they now repel the slightest provocation.[16]

The editor not only ascribed blame to his countrymen, but also to the government of Panama:

the government ot Panama is to blame for this—they should have protected their citizens when abused—if they had done this, nearly every foreigner in this country would have aided them. [The government's] weakness and imbecility has been the cause of all the trouble and riots and bloodshed which have occurred.[17]

As the *Yanquis* looked about Panama City, they realized that they were a good distance from Philadelphia or Charleston both in miles and in the comforts of home. If, as we assume, most of the travelers were eastern city-dwellers (or they would not have been able to afford the passage), they were accustomed to certain conveniences that had become necessities for them. We can understand why they would object to the rather untidy conditions of the streets and places of business. A newspaperman couched his opinion in these terms:

We would respectfully suggest to the City Authorities the propriety —indeed, the necessity, of immediately adopting some means, effectually to purify the city from the filth of every description which is accumulating so rapidly that it is not only excessively offensive to the senses but highly prejudicial to the health of the place. It is hardly possible for a person not acquainted with Panama to conceive the wretched, disgusting and dangerous condition of the streets and walls of the city.[18]

Following this, the author claimed that improvement should be expected because the government collected one dollar specifically for sanitation from each foreigner who crossed the Isthmus. Since cholera was raging nearby, one can understand the newspaperman's concern. Others suggested additional changes that needed to be instituted by the local government. The editor of the *Star* said that if changes were not made, then

it may become necessary for those located here to protect themselves. Whenever this may be—and perhaps the time is not distant—all well-disposed citizens and strangers will be forced to rise as one man to put down anarchy and establish a strong, fearless government, make just laws, abolish all unfair taxation, establish Jury trials and enforce PEACE AND ORDER.[19]

An ordinance designed to alleviate the unsanitary conditions was issued and made public on June 7, 1850. It required merchants and residents to put barrels in front of their doors for the collection of debris and refuse. These were to be emptied periodically by the city authorities.[20] The requirement for a general improvement in sanitation helped to eliminate other disagreeable conditions. Prior to the action there were a number of stalls where ginger pop, coffee, fruits, and sweetmeats were sold. The editor of the English-language paper attacked them as "a perfect nuisance [which] . . . produce more sickness from the quantity of filth around them than [all] other things combined." [21] Following the passage of the new ordinance these booths were eliminated.

The *Star* indicated that two *Yanquis,* with a view to supplying a needed service as well as making a few dollars, had an idea for a water supply. Messrs. Burnham and Sanford obtained from the authorities of Panama a grant giving them the exclusive right of supply. They proposed the formation of a joint-stock company with a one hundred thousand dollar capitalization and shares selling for fifty dollars.[22] At least a few people were doing something about local conditions besides complaining.

An item always most dear to the person away from home is mail. The receipt of it was usually irregular in the days before modern mail service, but the *Yanqui* felt that he was being persecuted by the local authorities when certain modifications were made in the distribution of mails. The system as it first was established provided for the United States consul to receive the incoming mail, remove letters addressed to him and to his countrymen residing in Panama, and then send the rest to California. This arrangement was ended when "owing either to the stupid perverseness of some local official or to the malicious intermeddling of some mischeivous [*sic*] busy body," [23] a new method was begun. Under the new system the mail had to be bundled by the local post office and the letters were placed in an open box where they were to be "abandoned to the examination of anyone who may expect a letter, or who has nothing better to do." It was claimed in some cases that the letters were entirely worn out from constant handling. The *Yanquis* viewed the whole episode as a deliberate affront. It was felt that the *Panameños*

> would not have acted in this matter, in a manner calculated to convey the impression that they never leave unimproved every opportunity that presents [itself] to gratify a national or personal feeling of bitter animosity towards our North American people.[24]

The remedy proposed was to protest to the United States Government. But an editor of the *Star* said, "In the meantime we must rest content with the present state of things under the dog-in-the-manger policy of the sapient authorities of Panama." [25]

Business, however, tended to encourage friendly relations. *Pana-meño* and *Yanqui* businessmen did have a common meeting ground, maybe not of the minds but, at least, of the pocketbooks. They became dependent upon each other for certain goods and services. Most advertisements were listed in both languages, and it can be assumed that many direct business contacts were made. The *Pana-meño* may not have developed tastes for *Yanqui* mattresses, tea, and pastries—they were too expensive—but "segars," flour, and several other products were desired. The *Yanqui* used native ropes, fruits, woods, and other forest products. Natives of the isthmus resented competition which interfered with profitable monopolies. This is implied in a notice that all interpreting had to be done by the public interpreter appointed by the governor. One can assume, however, that economic contacts were for the most part amicable, perhaps by necessity.

Some social functions were also enjoyed by both cultural groups. It is doubtful that many *Panameños* attended the Reverend Mr. Williams's Protestant religious services, conducted each Sunday in the spacious dining hall of the American Hotel,[26] but there were other opportunities for the groups to intermingle. The arrival of Mr. and Mrs. Charles Thorn with their "talented theatrical corps" probably brought a few of the *Panameños* to the hotel dining room to hear some of the "old standard English comedies." [27] Colonel Mann's circus company, which arrived in town in the second week of June 1850 doubtless drew crowds of fun-seekers.[28] North Americans were sometimes encouraged by their countrymen to use the public baths, which were judged to be "excellent and necessary to health in [that] time." Also, the primitive (but unexplained) construction of the baths fascinated the *Yanqui* bathers.[29] Another social event, unplanned but attended by a crowd of spectators in the cathedral plaza, was an impromptu fight between two horses. The rearing and neighing of the horses were augmented by the barking of dogs, who seemed eager to make the duet into a concert. The contest ended when the gray horse inflicted a telling bite on the neck of the black horse, and the latter took flight. The throng followed the action for several blocks but dispersed when it became apparent that the black horse had been defeated.[30]

The editorial commentary of both Spanish-language and English-language papers occasionally suggested a unanimity of opinion on certain events. The reporting of the Fourth of July celebration in

1850 is a good example. Both papers describe in glowing terms the 6:00 A.M. procession of several hundred people from the front of the American Hotel to the governor's house; to the residences of the French, British, and American consuls, then to the hotel for a banquet, where dozens of toasts were drunk in honor of practically every known statesman, and even to "the girls we left behind." The paper *El Panameño* concluded its summary on the celebration by saying, "At last, when night fell no person returned to his quarters with the memory of any dismal or disagreeable occurrences, and there existed only the feeling of the union and friendship between North Americans and New Granadians." [31] Is it possible that while the *Panameños* were merely having a good time, the *Yanquis* were expressing devoted patriotism?

There were times when the papers carried on running verbal battles. The *Star* invariably supported the policies and the reputation of the United States consul, Mr. Amos Corwine, who had

> commanded a company of rifles in Col. Davis' regiment at the battle of Buena Vista and was honorably mentioned in the report of his colonel, for having maintained his position with fearful odds against him, although wounded in action.[32]

However, when Corwine returned to the United States in June 1850, for business reasons connected with his commission and supply house, *El Panameño* announced that he had been recalled to give an account of his conduct. It said that this recall showed "an evidence of the disposition of our [Panamanian] government to render justice and satisfaction to the Granadian people." The *Star*, in rejoinder, declared that Corwine had not been recalled and that the Panamanians should feel more indebted to Corwine for peace and calm than to any other one person, "their governor and his barefooted soldiers not excepted." [33]

The Spanish- and the English-language papers defended each other at times. In June 1850, for example, the *Star* praised *El Panameño* for its fairness and for the fact that it had doubled its circulation within the past year. *El Panameño* reciprocated when it rebutted a statement in *El Comercio* (Lima, Peru) concerning *Yanqui* complaints in regard to Isthmian climate and health.[34]

The rapid turnover of publishers of the *Star* undoubtedly contributed considerably to the hot and cold attitudes expressed by the paper towards Panama. That publishers also succumbed to the gold fever

was shown when *El Panameño* wished a *bon voyage* to a Mr. Bidde-
man, the editor responsible for the first three numbers of the *Star*,
and to Messrs. Henarie and Bachman, responsible for the fourth issue
—all in the same article.[35]

Thus the newspapers of Panama recorded the impact of the Forty-
Niner and his culture upon the Isthmus during his early contacts en
route to the California gold fields. At that time the United States did
not seem too interested in the annexation of Panamanian territory,
but continued to express satisfaction with the Bidlack treaty of 1846
in which it guaranteed New Granada's sovereignty over the province
in return for the right of passage across the Isthmus. Señor Líevano
y Alejo Morales of New Granada suggested that the Isthmus should
be sold to the United States for ten million pesos because "sooner or
later we'll lose it anyway." The United States-owned paper *Panama
Echo*, took issue with him:

> Sell your country! and be the mockery . . . of the whole world! To
> be an abhorrent seducer, and called the Iscariot of the nations! Oh!
> what a shame would be descended to our children! . . . .

> The United States does not have the need nor the wish to buy your
> country. They have too much territory. They are strong and you are
> weak . . . and if anyone comes to invade you, and you need assistance,
> it will not be necessary to say it twice. . . .[36]

Ironically, a little more than half a century after these words Theo-
dore Roosevelt was to state: "I took the Canal Zone and let the Congress debate, and while the debate goes on, the Canal does also." [37]

The bold steps taken in the early twentieth century extended
United States domination to the very borders of South America. The
early penetration by the Forty-Niners, as much as any one other
thing, helped to lay the groundwork for that expansion.

Notes

1. Albert Z. Carr, *The World and William Walker* (New York:
Harper & Row, 1963), passim. This is the most recent and very readable
account of this adventurer.

2. Mary W. Williams, *Anglo-American Isthmian Diplomacy, 1815–
1915* (New York: Russell and Russell, 1965), p. 53.

3. James K. Polk, *The Diary of James K. Polk, 1845–1849*, ed. M. M.
Quaife, 4 vols. (Chicago, 1910), vol. 1, p. 71 as quoted by Williams,
Anglo-American Isthmian Diplomacy, pp. 53–54.

4. E. Taylor Parks, *Colombia and the United States, 1765–1934* (Dur-

ham, N.C.: Duke University Press, 1935), pp. 202–215. The puzzle involved was why had Britain not accepted the offer of New Granada three years before when it was presented and why had three years elapsed before the offer was made to the United States.

5. Ibid., p. 210.

6. Ray A. Billington, *The Far Western Frontier* (New York: Harper & Row, 1956), pp. 224 and 277. Billington quotes John H. Kemble's "Pacific Mail Service between Panama and San Francisco, 1849–1851," *Pacific Historical Review* (1933), vol. 2, pp. 405–417.

7. Ibid., p. 225. The first mailboat bound for San Francisco had reached Panama City on Jan. 17, 1849, and over 1,000 persons had vied for the 250 spaces available. Actually 365 crammed aboard and one paid as much as $1,000 for steerage accommodations.

8. *Star*, Feb. 24, 1849. The *Star* was an English-language newspaper published in the city of Panama.

9. Ibid., Mar. 29, 1850.

10. Ibid., Apr. 6, 1850.

11. Ibid.

12. Ibid.

13. Ibid., June 29, 1850.

14. *El Panameño*, July 14, 1850. The article was headed "Chagres Granadino y Chagres Norte Americano."

15. *Star*, Mar. 29, 1850.

16. Ibid., June 7, 1850.

17. Ibid.

18. Ibid., Apr. 6, 1850.

19. Ibid., June 7, 1850.

20. Ibid., Apr. 6, 1850.

21. Ibid., June 7, 1850.

22. Ibid.

23. Ibid., Mar. 29, 1850.

24. Ibid., Apr. 6, 1850.

25. Ibid.

26. Ibid., Feb. 24, 1849.

27. Ibid., Apr. 19, 1850.

28. Ibid., June 7, 1850.

29. Ibid., July 13, 1850.

30. Ibid., July 20, 1850.

31. *El Panameño*, July 7, 1850.

32. *Star*, Apr. 19, 1850.

33. As reported in the *Star*, Apr. 19, 1850.

34. *Star*, Mar. 17, 1849.

35. *El Panameño*, Mar. 18, 1849.

36. As reported in *El Panameño*, June 23, 1850.

37. Samuel F. Bemis, *A Diplomatic History of the United States* (New York: Henry Holt and Company, 1942), p. 517.

5 | Southern Baptists in Cuba, 1886-1916

Harold Edward Greer, Jr.

The Roman Catholic religion has exercised a profound influence on the history and culture of Latin America. Since the beginning of the nineteenth century, however, Protestantism has also made a significant impact on the region. Many Protestant missionaries, in addition to their doctrinal teachings, fostered such concepts as religious freedom, separation of Church and State, and education for all citizens. Certain liberals of Latin America shared these aims and often extended their support to Protestant denominations. Most of the missionary work was sponsored by Protestant churches in the United States, and, therefore, was related to the growing influence of that nation throughout Latin America.

Cuba became one of the most important fields of Protestant activity, largely because of its proximity to the United States. Many denominations shared in this movement, but one of the most active was the Southern Baptists. A study of this group and its activities in Cuba from 1886 to 1916 will serve as a case study of Protestant influence in Latin America. At the same time it will give further insight into Cuban history and the complex relationship between that nation and the United States during a very significant period.

The people of Cuba had given nominal allegiance to Roman Catholicism ever since the island was colonized by Spain. However, Catholic churches were never so widespread in Cuba as in other countries of Latin America such as Mexico and Peru. Many of the priests and nuns were of Spanish birth, reflecting the continued colonial status of the island after most Latin American nations had won their independence in the early nineteenth century. Allied with the Spanish government and with those who desired to maintain the status quo, the Roman Catholic Church alienated liberals and others who advocated Cuban independence.[1] This prevailing attitude toward the

Catholic Church helped to make it possible for Protestants to move into Cuba. The Spanish government, though closely allied with the Catholic Church, allowed Protestants to organize missionary work on the island. Besides Southern Baptists, the Presbyterians, Methodists, Episcopalians, and Jamaican Baptists established missions in Cuba well before the Spanish-American War.

The initial efforts of the Southern Baptist Convention in Cuba resulted from the leadership of the Reverend William Wood, missionary pastor in Key West, Florida. After a Cuban family joined his church in 1884, the minister became interested in doing mission work among the Cubans in Key West and in Cuba itself. At Wood's request the Florida Baptist Convention voted in 1884 to begin work among the almost five thousand Cubans at Key West. Converts of this mission who returned home sent back word of a man named Alberto J. Díaz who was preaching Baptist doctrines to large congregations in Havana. Following instructions of the Florida Board of Missions, Wood traveled to Havana to meet the preacher.[2] This contact proved to be an important one, for Alberto Díaz was to lead Southern Baptist work in Cuba for the next fifteen years.

Díaz had fled from his native island during the Ten Years' War, an unsuccessful revolt against Spanish rule which took place from 1868 to 1878. As a refugee in New York he had attended Baptist services, and, during a subsequent visit to that city in 1882, had been baptized and trained by the Reverend R. B. Montgomery. A short time later the new convert returned to his native island as a colporteur of the American Bible Society.[3] Some Cubans responded to his preaching and organized a church based on the teachings of the New Testament. This was the group William F. Wood found when he went to Havana.[4] Díaz was ordained December 13, 1885 in the First Baptist Church of Key West.[5] He and his sister, Minnie Díaz, became the first Southern Baptist missionaries to Cuba, appointed by the Florida Board of Missions.[6]

Wood and Díaz together organized the missionary effort. Wood described the first Baptist baptism in Cuba, which took place on January 20, 1886:

> On Wednesday night, with Brother Alberto, we went to meeting in Havana. At the close of the service we went by twos, and very quietly wending our way through the streets, we came to the sea, and there, by the light of the moon, in an obscure place, we baptized three believers, the first fruits unto God of this mission in Havana,

Cuba. Then, scattering as we came, went to our homes. God's holy name be praised for this beginning.[7]

Other baptisms which followed were, like this one, performed in secret, because Spanish law forbade any act of non-Catholic worship outside a building.[8] On January 26, 1886, the group of baptized believers of Havana organized themselves into the first Baptist congregation in Cuba, the Gethsemane Baptist Church.[9] The following May, the Southern Baptist Convention voted to accept the work initiated in Cuba by the Florida Board of Missions and assigned the field to its Home Mission Board.[10] Within a year the membership of the Gethsemane congregation had increased to 133.[11] Two years later, in the spring of 1888, the Home Mission Board listed in its annual report 1,100 members in six churches and nineteen preaching stations in Cuba.[12]

The rapid growth of the Baptist mission work was related to the political conditions that prevailed in Cuba during the last decade of the nineteenth century. Dr. Isaac Taylor Tichenor, executive secretary of the Southern Baptist Home Mission Board, made several trips to Cuba to supervise church activities and found that the Liberal Party on the island approved the Baptist work and principles. This party, in view of the alliance between the Roman Catholic Church and the Spanish government, stood for the separation of Church and State. One Liberal leader told Tichenor that the Baptist Church was, in his opinion, an object lesson for the Cuban people. The Havana press, which strongly opposed the existing ecclesiastical and political system, sympathized with the Baptist work. Tichenor felt that the alleged corruption and immorality of some Catholic priests also worked to the advantage of Protestantism.[13] J. V. Cova, one of the outstanding Cuban Baptist preachers, expressed the opinion that many Cubans preferred the Baptist Church because they looked upon the Catholic Church as a spiritual oppressor. Many called it the "Spanish Church," for most priests were imported from Spain, and they "could hardly write and never preached." Cova stated that the Cubans liked the simplicity of the Baptist meetings and that the Baptists had a reputation for being honest people who rendered their services without charge.[14]

Baptists strengthened their work in Havana in the fall of 1888, when the Home Mission Board purchased the spacious Jané Theater building for sixty-five thousand dollars.[15] The theater, a stone structure seating three thousand persons, stood on a corner near the Prado in the finest part of the city.[16] The purchase of this building led the people of Havana to have greater confidence in the stability and permanence of the Baptist work.[17]

Spanish governmental regulations caused some difficulties for Protestant groups prior to the Spanish-American War. Spanish law required that Protestant worship be held behind closed doors and windows in order not to attract attention.[18] In 1890, a permanent inspector was appointed to examine all Baptist places of worship to make sure each meeting room was large enough for the number of people attending.[19] The same year police interrupted Baptist services at Guanabacoa and arrested three ministers, who were charged with holding a meeting in a building not legally classified as a chapel. The courts later declared the three preachers were not guilty and dismissed the case.[20] Regulations were not always strictly enforced, and Protestants were frequently allowed to open their doors and windows, and newspapers willingly made announcements of their meetings.[21] By 1892, Southern Baptist Church property was exempt from taxation, just as was the property of the Catholic Church.[22]

Although the Protestant groups enjoyed a relatively favorable position under the Spanish colonial administration, they faced opposition from other sources. Creating and operating a Baptist cemetery was a major source of conflict. Such a facility was urgently needed, because Protestants could not be buried in Catholic cemeteries. Purchase of six acres for use as a burial ground was made possible in January, 1887 by contributions from the Alabama Baptist Convention and from Mr. J. S. Payne, a Baptist businessman from Boston who wintered in Cuba.[23] The new cemetery was widely used, and in 1888 it was said that one-third of the city was burying its dead there.[24] This trend was irksome to the Catholic clergy in Cuba, for whom income from burials was a major source of revenue. The bishop of Havana, having unsuccessfully opposed the licensing of the Baptist cemetery, continued to attack it by all means at his disposal, denouncing it from the pulpit and in publications. The only road to the cemetery, which crossed Catholic property, was obstructed and on at least two occasions priests were alleged to have interfered with Baptist funerals.[25]

Despite the inconveniences caused by such opposition, Baptist activities increased rapidly in the years prior to the Spanish-American War. Sunday Schools and day schools soon supplemented the mission work. Since the government had neglected education for the poorer classes, the free Baptist schools could not accommodate all the children who applied for admission.[26] In 1894 E. Pendleton Jones, who had gone to Cuba as a missionary the previous year, listed five coeducational Baptist schools in Cuba and one girls' school. There were 440 students and 13 teachers in all the schools.[27] A typical Sunday School was that of the Gethsemane Baptist Church in Havana. It met for an hour and a half, and the pupils studied Bible assignments.[28] In 1894 there were seven Sunday Schools with a total of 1,000 pupils and teachers.[29] Almost all the Baptist work was done by native Cubans, their number having reached 24 by 1895.[30] The only exception to this was E. Pendleton Jones, and he was forced to return to the United States after only six months because of illness.[31]

The revolutionary movement against Spain, which began in 1895, greatly affected the missionary work in Cuba. Most Baptist workers withdrew from the island by 1896 and went to the United States to continue their religious efforts among Cubans there. Missionary work on the island was continued by Cuban converts, among them Alberto Díaz is of special interest. He participated in the revolt against Spain and served as commander-in-chief of the insurgent forces in Havana Province. These revolutionary activities led to his arrest by government officials. But after a popular outcry from influential Baptists in the United States, Washington exerted pressure and secured Díaz's release.[32]

The Spanish-American War represented a major turning point in the history of Cuba, reshaping its economic and social institutions as well as assisting in its break from Spanish control. The United States exercised far-reaching influence on the island, establishing a virtual protectorate there. It is in the light of this new situation that religious conditions after 1898 must be viewed. Immediately after the conflict, Protestantism was received enthusiastically. One American chaplain, D. H. Parker, gave his opinion of the religious situation in Cuba: "Here is the ripest field on earth, I suppose. . . . Rome is dead here; she has no place in the hearts of many people."[33] Equally optimistic for the Protestant cause was a statement made in Santa Clara Province by another United States chaplain, E. W. White.

> The idea of liberty is so attractive to these people that they grasp at the principle of religious liberty and the congregational system of church life, as a drowning man clutches at the life line in mid-ocean.

They have had enough of one man power in religion as well as politics.[34]

Southern Baptists resumed their activities following the signing of an armistice between the United States and Spain. José R. O'Halloran, a Cuban pastor before the war, was sent to Santiago and began mission activities there September 30, 1898. His work in Santiago expanded rapidly and was extended to Guantánamo following a request by Chaplain D. H. Parker. By the end of 1898 O'Halloran had baptized 150 believers and had organized two churches.[35] In Santa Clara Province Chaplain E. W. White aided the Baptist mission work during the United States occupation.[36]

The Presbyterians, Methodists, and Episcopalians also reopened their Cuban work following cessation of hostilities. They were joined by new groups, including the Congregationalists, Disciples of Christ, Quakers, and American (Northern) Baptists.[37] Since both the American Baptist Home Mission Society and the Southern Baptist Home Mission Board were interested in Cuba and Puerto Rico, a meeting was planned to discuss a division of these mission fields. Committees representing the two groups met in Washington, D.C. on November 23, 1898. An agreement was reached whereby Puerto Rico and the two eastern provinces of Cuba—Oriente and Camagüey—were designated as fields for the American Baptists. Southern Baptists were assigned the four western provinces of Cuba—Matanzas, Havana, Pinar del Río, and Santa Clara.[38]

In many instances Baptist workers received aid and encouragement from the Cuban officials. At Santa Clara the meetings were often crowded, with people of high standing in the community attending the services. A theater was loaned to the Baptists free of charge, and one of the papers gave them the free use of its columns.[39] A general in the town of Cabarién offered the use of his house, and the mayor of Camajuaní allowed the Baptists to preach in the town hall.[40] The mayor, General Clemente Gómez, and the city council prepared a meeting place and took part in special Baptist services conducted at Jovellanos.[41] Reasons for Protestant popularity at this time were suggested by the head of the American Baptist work in eastern Cuba:

> The people gladly hear the gospel, our preaching halls are crowded at every service. The Cubans, however, have no idea of spiritual religion; they are nominally Catholics, but care little for their religion. I should say that nine-tenths of them are indifferent. They come to

hear us preach, because it is something new and they are attracted by the novelty. They have little reverence, and are densely ignorant of even the most superficial knowledge of the Bible. We could receive and baptize hundreds of them who are disgusted with Romanism, but who know nothing of real heart religion. They disclaim being Catholics, remembering the attitude of the Romish church during their struggle for liberty from the yoke of Spain. Two men came to see me yesterday to tell me that they were going to "enter our religion," as they express it. I questioned them and found that they had never attended services nor read the Bible, but they wanted to "enter your religion" because they were Cuban patriots, and hated the Romish church.[42]

Immediately after the Spanish-American War, the Protestants not only enjoyed a favorable position with the general population but also were greatly assisted by acts of the newly established Cuban government.[43] For example, Protestants were put on an equal footing with Catholics in regard to marriage as a result of the following decree:

The Civil Marriage Contract: The Military Government has just decided that all the marriages that occur, whatever be the religious sect under whose auspices they may take place, shall be valid and recorded in the civil register. The municipal judge shall always sanction it with his presence.[44]

Of even greater significance was a provision in the constitution of the newly established Cuban republic which went into effect on May 20, 1902. This provision guaranteed the rights of Protestants on the island in the following terms:

The profession of all religions is free, as well as the exercise of all cults without limitation, except that they must respect Christian morality and public order. The Church will be separated from the State, and in no case will it subsidize any cult.[45]

The Southern Baptist Home Mission Board took advantage of the favorable situation. Making use of its cadre of Cuban preachers, converted before the war, it increased its activities in all four western provinces. O'Halloran turned over his Santiago field to the American Baptists and began work in Cienfuegos. Cova established work at Matanzas, and Gaspar de Cárdenas, a member of the first group baptized in Cuba, began work in Pinar del Río in 1900. The board rehired Alberto Díaz as missionary in Havana and as pastor of the

Gethsemane Baptist Church.[46] New workers were also sent to the island. In 1901 the board was able to employ C. D. Daniel, who had worked under the Baptist Foreign Mission Board in Brazil and under the Texas State Board among the Mexicans.[47]

The optimism which had been expressed by Protestants just after the Spanish-American War and the initial successes experienced under changed circumstances did not long continue. The conduct of some of the Americans occupying Cuba was not of a quality to recommend the United States government, customs, or religion.[48] Daniel described many of the soldiers as being an "irreligious, immoral, lewd, drunken crowd of fellows, who assume the air of conquerors and frequently boast that the stars and stripes will never be taken from Cuba." [49] The friction between Cubans and Americans increased to such a point that it hindered the mission work. Cuban newspapers charged that the United States did not intend to fulfill its promise to give Cuba its liberty.[50] The strained relations in 1901 over the Platt Amendment increased the tension. The Cubans resented the pressure requiring them to accept the document, especially Article 3 which gave the United States the right of intervention. They felt this clause in effect destroyed Cuban independence.[51]

The Cuban-American friction affected Baptist mission work directly when trouble developed between Alberto Díaz and the Home Mission Board. In the election of 1900, held to choose delegates to the Cuban Constitutional Convention, the veteran Baptist minister from Havana made speeches for the Cuban National Party, in which he opposed the United States activities on the island.[52] His suspicion of American intentions was made clear in a communication with a member of the Home Mission Board, in which he asked if the southern and western people were "in favor of Platt's amendment on annexation of Cuba to U.S." [53] In the spring and summer of 1901 Díaz was an active political candidate, turning his pulpit over to a substitute preacher who was opposed by various Baptists. The Reverend Mr. Daniel expressed the opinion that the Cuban minister had hurt the mission effort because of his vile statements against political opponents.[54] The Mission Board's Committee on Cuba wrote to Díaz acknowledging its sympathy for the feelings of the Cuban people, but reminding him of the Baptists' long belief in the separation of Church and State, and in keeping political matters out of the churches. The individual had every right to his views, but the Church should not become involved in politics or be used for political purposes.[55] As a result of this letter, Díaz resigned on May 9, 1901.[56]

Despite Díaz's resignation as its missionary, the board allowed the Gethsemane Church to continue under his pastorate using the Jané Theater building. In the spring of 1903, however, Díaz and the Gethsemane Church filed suit claiming the Jané property.[57] The suit dragged on for a long time, but was finally decided in favor of the Home Mission Board in January, 1907 by the Supreme Court of Cuba.[58] The suit was very costly to the board; further, it hurt the work in Havana. A new Baptist church was organized in the city on January 24, 1902 made up of twenty members, both Cubans and Americans, some of whom had been members of the Gethsemane Church. The new church took the name Calvary Baptist Church, and Daniel served as its pastor.[59]

Taking advantage of suspicions on the part of the Cuban population, the Catholic officials represented the Baptists and other Protestants as serving the political views of the "Yankee" government of Cuba. After United States troops ended their occupation, the Catholics pointed out that all "the Americans" had left Cuba except the Protestant missionaries. The goal of these missionaries, according to the priests, was to "Americanize" the Cubans so that they would eventually desire annexation to the United States. The Catholic Church appealed to the Cubans to preserve their sacred heritage: their race, their language, and their religion.[60]

Suspicion and resentment against the United States continued to be influential factors in hindering the missionary effort. In 1912, when the United States threatened to intervene in Cuba under the Platt Amendment, a Baptist visitor to Cuba reported that there was an almost universal feeling of anxiety and resentment among the islanders. One Cuban government official explained:

We fear no nation in the world except the United States; no other nation can interfere with us, for we are under your protection; but we do really fear intervention by your government, for we know that means the loss of our independence so dear to our hearts.[61]

Despite the problems within their own ranks, and the suspicions related to political conditions, the Baptist increased their activities in Cuba from 1901 to 1916. The time was past when a missionary's presence in a town was a new and sensational event. He no longer provoked any special emotions. Persons attended services for spiritual reasons, rather than from curiosity or other motives. Missionaries reported that converts seemed to be standing firmer.[62] An outstanding group of Cuban Baptist pastors helped to stimulate this growth. One of the most prominent was J. V. Cova, a literary figure who translated a number of books into Spanish and edited a Baptist newspaper. Another, R. R. Machado, earned his LL.D. degree at the University of Havana, and became well known as a lawyer, poet, newspaper columnist, orator, and preacher. Dr. Eduardo Francisco Rodríguez, who had studied medicine in the United States, France, and Spain, served as Baptist pastor for many years without pay while continuing his medical practice. Other important Cuban workers included A. U. Cabrera, M. M. Calejo, and A. T. Bequer.[63]

The need for capable, permanent leadership for the mission in Cuba was met in January 1905, when the Home Mission Board appointed Moses Nathaniel McCall, a former public school principal and pastor from Georgia. Later that year C. D. Daniel retired, leaving McCall, still new in the work, to head the Southern Baptist mission in Cuba. Plagued by a constant turnover of workers, many of whom discovered that they could not maintain good health in the climate, the Board found in McCall a man determined to remain in Cuba to which he believed God had sent him. Even after the tragic death of his wife, which left him with four small children, McCall persevered. He even remained at his post after two of his children contracted tuberculosis and were forced to seek a more favorable climate in the United States. McCall continued as superintendent of the Cuban mission for forty-two years until his death in 1947.[64]

With the relatively favorable political conditions, a staff of dedicated preachers, and the leadership of Moses McCall, the Southern Baptists turned their attention to other problems, such as the need for church buildings to house the various congregations. Not only were rents unreasonably high, but most rented halls, lacking the appearance of churches, had little appeal to the Cubans. In the Cuban city of Trinidad, the Baptists were called "birds of passage" because they owned no church building.[65] It was felt by leaders that if the churches acquired property, it would give them the appearance of permanence.[66] Many of them also felt that if some calamity should separate the Cubans from United States aid, owning church property would make it easier for the Cubans to perpetuate the work.[67] Convinced of this need, the Home Mission Board began in 1904 to buy suitable lots on which to build churches in the towns where missionary activities were under way. This led to the construction of church buildings and pastors' homes in most of these towns, and school facilities in many of them.[68]

Educational activities proved to be one of the most successful aspects of Southern Baptist work. The day school program, initiated before the Spanish-American War, increased rapidly after 1901, and by 1913 there were ten mission day schools.[69] The most outstanding school sponsored by the Southern Baptists was the Cuban-American College of Havana, which opened in 1906 with a faculty of six.[70] This institution included classes from kindergarten through high school and offered two years of college. It conformed to all the requirements of the Cuban Department of Education; its graduates were therefore eligible to take the official examination leading to the A.B. degree given by the National Institute of Cuba.[71] In connection with the Cuban-American College, M. N. McCall began a seminary in 1906 for the instruction of young men preparing for the ministry. These ministerial students lived with the McCall family and were employed by the board as student missionaries.[72] One of the outstanding students in this seminary was Federico Rodríguez, a young man from the Canary Islands who was ordained in 1909 and employed as McCall's assistant in Havana. Rodríguez was a brick mason by trade and a man with an unusual capacity for hard work. He saw that Cuba needed Christian education because the public school system was inadequate. He organized a self-supporting boarding school, an action undertaken without assistance from any mission board. At one time the school had six hundred students, and it won repeated recognition for its contribution to education. It became the model for several such schools established by the Cuban government.[73]

In 1905 the Baptist churches of western Cuba formed a convention. Officially named the Convention of the Baptist Church of the Four Occidental Provinces in Cooperation with the Home Mission Board of the Southern Baptist Convention, it was popularly referred to as the West Cuba Baptist Convention.[74] The formation of this body stimulated Baptist work and facilitated the development of a strong *denomination* in western Cuba. In 1907 publication of a denominational paper was begun, and in 1911 the West Cuba Baptist Sunday School Association promoted the use of teaching methods that had been proved successful by Southern Baptists in the United States. One of the Cuban ministers translated into Spanish the *Normal*

Handbook for Sunday School Workers.[75] In 1913, the Cuban Woman's Missionary Union was organized in association with the convention.[76]

The year 1916 marked the thirtieth anniversary of Southern Baptist work in Cuba. In that year there were twenty-seven missionaries, all but three of whom were Cubans, supplying forty-three churches and stations. Sunday School enrollment had reached 2,507, and in the previous year 1,033 Bibles and Testaments had been distributed. During that time the Cuban Baptists had contributed $4,065.82 to church work. The church membership in 1916 was only 1,896, but the total number of converts since the beginning of missionary activities had been much higher, many having died or moved away. By 1916 the Home Mission Board had spent $242,250.00 on property in Cuba.[77]

It is impossible to measure the total impact of Southern Baptist work in Cuba, for membership statistics do not indicate true influences on Cuban society as a whole. The Baptists claimed partial credit for a quickening of intellectual life and the creation of an improved civic atmosphere. They likewise contributed to the improvement of hygiene and sanitation, as the missionaries gave needed instruction in matters of health. After the legalization of Protestant marriages (which were performed without charge), there was a substantial reduction in the number of Cubans who were living together in common-law marriages.

The Baptists and their fellow Protestants did not succeed in winning the Cuban masses to their cause, and the predictions for the collapse of the Roman Catholic Church that had been made following the defeat of Spain failed to materialize. The failure was partly related to the growing resentment against the United States on political and economic grounds. Ironically, the victory over Spain, which had opened the doors of Cuba to increased Protestant activity, also strengthened the Catholic Church in its appeal to the islanders. Having broken the political ties with Spain, Cubans gained a new appreciation for the cultural heritage that had linked them for four centuries with the mother country. The Roman Catholic Church, a basic part of that tradition, retained its position as a major force in Cuban society. The removal of its privileged status seemed detrimental at first, but in the long run tended to give it new strength. Certain Protestants felt that their competition stimulated the Catholics to serve more effectively.[78]

However, alongside the Catholic Church stood strong new religious groups, including the Southern Baptists. There was no longer the close tie between Cuban liberals and Protestant leaders, but the fact that they had supported each other at a crucial time in the history of the island was not forgotten. By 1916, the Southern Baptists were firmly established in Cuba and constituted a significant element in the complex society of the new Republic.

Notes

1. Kenneth Scott Latourette, *Advance through Storm, A History of the Expansion of Christianity*, 7 vols., (New York: Harper and Brothers, 1945), vol. 7, pp. 175–176.
2. H. M. King, "Origin of the Cuban Work," *Our Home Field* (March, 1889), vol. 1, p. 6.
3. J. William Jones, "Sketch of Rev. A. J. Díaz, 'The Apostle of Cuba,'" *The Seminary Magazine* (April 1896), vol. 9, pp. 349–353; and R. B. Montgomery, Feb. 23, 1893, *Our Home Field* (March 1893), vol. 5, p. 5. In instances such as this where no addressee is given, it is assumed that the letter is addressed either to the periodical or to someone who then turned it over to the periodical.
4. Isaac Taylor Tichenor, "Cuba," *Our Home Field* (August 1888), vol. 5, p. 2.
5. William F. Wood, Dec. 19, 1885, *Christian Index* (Jan. 14, 1886), vol. 64, p. 4.
6. King, "Origin of the Cuban Work," p. 6.
7. Wood, Jan. 23, 1886, *Christian Index* (Feb. 14, 1886), vol. 64, p. 4.
8. Ibid.
9. Jones, "Sketch of Rev. A. J. Díaz," pp. 349–353.
10. *Proceedings, Thirty-First Session, Forty-First Year, of the Southern Baptist Convention* (Atlanta, 1886), pp. 13, 21, 29 (hereinafter cited as *Proceedings*).
11. A. J. Díaz to Home Mission Board, Jan. 24, 1887, "Third Quarterly Report of Mission in Cuba," *Christian Index* (Feb. 17, 1887), vol. 65, p. 3.
12. *Proceedings*, (1888), pp. i, vi.
13. Tichenor, "A Second Visit to Cuba," *Our Home Field* (December, 1888), vol. 1, pp. 6–7; and Tichenor, "Matters in Cuba," *Christian Index* (Jan. 12, 1893), vol. 70, p. 7.
14. J. V. Cova to editor, Jan. 12, 1892, *Christian Index* (Jan. 28, 1892), vol. 69, p. 2; and Cova, n.d., *Christian Index* (Dec. 8, 1892), vol. 69, p. 5.
15. Minutes, Nov. 23, 1888, Home Mission Board of the Southern Baptist Convention (MS in files of the Home Mission Board, Atlanta, hereinafter cited as Minutes).
16. "The Havana Building Bought by the Home Board," *Christian Index* (July 25, 1889), vol. 66, p. 6.
17. Tichenor, "House of Worship in Havana," *Christian Index* (Dec.

6, 1888), vol. 65, p. 3; and Lansing Burrows, "The Havana Church," *Christian Index* (Mar. 31, 1892), vol. 69, p. 6.

18. Tichenor, "Another Visit to Cuba," *Our Home Field* (March 1889), vol. 1, p. 5.

19. Díaz to Tichenor, July 26, 1890, *Our Home Field* (September 1890), vol. 3, pp. 2–3.

20. Díaz to Tichenor, n.d., *Christian Index* (July 10, 1890), vol. 67, p. 8.; Díaz to Consul General Ramon O. Williams, July 27, 1890, "The Recent Imprisonment of Our Missionaries in Guanabacoa," *Our Home Field* (September 1890), vol. 3, pp. 1–2.; and "The Latest from Cuba," *Our Home Field* (April 1891), vol. 3, p. 4.

21. Cova, Dec. 22, 1890, *Christian Index* (Jan. 15, 1891), vol. 68, p. 2; and Tichenor, "Another Visit to Cuba," p. 5.

22. Tichenor, "Matters in Cuba," *Christian Index* (Jan. 12, 1893), vol. 70, p. 7.

23. Díaz to Home Mission Board, Jan. 24, 1887, "Third Quarterly Report of Mission in Cuba," *Christian Index* (Feb. 17, 1887), vol. 65, p. 3; and "Cuba," *Our Home Field* (August 1888), vol. 1, p. 3.

24. Tichenor, "Visit to Cuba," *Christian Index* (Feb. 9, 1888), vol. 65, pp. 2–3.

25. J. William Jones, "Our Cuban Cemetery," June 19, 1888, *Christian Index* (June 28, 1888), vol. 65, p. 1; Tichenor, "A Second Visit to Cuba," pp. 6–7.; Díaz to Tichenor, July 2, 1888, "Cuba," *Our Home Field* (August 1888), vol. 1, p. 6; Díaz, n.d., "Persecution in Cuba," *Christian Index* (Aug. 23, 1888), vol. 65, p. 4; Cova to editor, Aug. 6, 1891, *Our Home Field* (September 1891), vol. 4, p. 3; and Cova, June 28, 1892, *Our Home Field* (August 1892), vol. 4, p. 1.

26. Cova to J. William Jones, Sept. 9, 1890, *Our Home Field* (October 1890), vol. 3, p. 2; and Cova, n.d., *Christian Index* (May 22, 1890), vol. 67, p. 12.

27. E. Pendleton Jones to Annie W. Armstrong, April 3, 1894, *Christian Index* (Aug. 9, 1894), vol. 71, p. 3.

28. E. Pendleton Jones to McConnell, Dec. 5, 1893, *Our Home Field* (February 1894), vol. 6, p. 2.

29. *Proceedings*, 1894, pp. lii, lvi.

30. *Proceedings*, 1895, pp. lxii, lxvi.

31. E. Pendleton Jones to Tichenor, *Our Home Field* (January, 1894), vol. 6, p. 2; and Minutes, Mar. 31, 1894.

32. Tichenor, account given at the 76th Annual Session of the Georgia Baptist State Convention, Mar. 31, 1898, *Christian Index* (April 7, 1898), vol. 78, p. 4; and M. M. Welch to McKinney, April 1, 1896, Letters of Welch (in files of the Home Mission Board).

33. D. H. Parker, n.d., *Christian Index* (Oct. 13, 1898), vol. 78, p. 5.

34. E. W. White to Tichenor, Mar. 5, 1899, *Christian Index* (Mar. 23, 1899), vol. 79, p. 5.

35. "Fifty-Fourth Annual Report of the Home Mission Board," *Annual of the Southern Baptist Convention*, 1899, pp. lxxx–lxxxi (herein-

after cited as *Annual*); and D. H. Parker, n.d., *Christian Index* (Oct. 13, 1898), vol. 78, p. 5.

36. White to Tichenor, Mar. 5, 1899, *Christian Index* (Mar. 23, 1899), vol. 79, p. 5.

37. Edward A. Odell, *It Came to Pass* (New York: Board of National Missions, Presbyterian Church in the U.S.A., 1952), pp. 79–80, 97–98; and *Havana Post*, Oct. 21, 1900.

38. Minutes, Dec. 6, 1898.

39. White to Tichenor, Mar. 5, 1899, *Christian Index* (Mar. 23, 1899), vol. 79, p. 5.

40. W. D. Powell, Mar. 5, 1899, *Christian Index* (Mar. 16, 1899), vol. 79, p. 5.

41. Cova to Welch, n.d., *Christian Index* (Aug. 31, 1899), vol. 79, p. 5.

42. H. R. Moseley, n.d., *Christian Index* (Mar. 15, 1900), vol. 80, p. 4.

43. *Annual*, 1899, p. lxxi.

44. "Marriages," *Our Home Field* (July, 1899), vol. 9, p. 2.

45. J. Lloyd Mecham, *Church and State in Latin America: A History of Politico-Ecclesiastical Relations* (Chapel Hill: University of North Carolina, 1934), p. 357.

46. Minutes, Jan. 17, 1899, Feb. 7, 1899, Apr. 6, 1899, and Mar. 3, 1900.

47. *Annual*, 1901, pp. 148–149.

48. Moseley, n.d., *Christian Index* (Mar. 15, 1900), vol. 80, p. 4.

49. Daniel to Tichenor, January, 1901, *Christian Index* (Jan. 31, 1901), vol. 81, p. 4.

50. Moseley, n.d., *Christian Index* (Mar. 15, 1900), vol. 80, p. 4.

51. David F. Healy, *The United States in Cuba, 1898–1902: Generals, Politicians, and the Search for Policy* (Madison, Wis.: University of Wisconsin Press, 1963), pp. 169, 170; and *Annual*, 1901, p. 148.

52. *Havana Post*, Sept. 23, 1900.

53. Díaz to Tichenor, Jan. 22, 1901 (in files of the Home Mission Board, Atlanta). The Platt Amendment did not contain such a provision as that intimated by Díaz.

54. Home Mission Board of the Southern Baptist Convention, *Statement on the Situation in Cuba* (Atlanta, 1903), p. 5; and C. D. Daniel, "Cuba," p. 19. This is a twenty-one page typewritten manuscript in the files of the Home Mission Board, Atlanta. Written in 1903, it is an answer to charges against the Southern Baptist work in Cuba made in other Baptist papers by Díaz. These papers printing Díaz's charges were of the Landmark Baptist group, which had broken from the Southern Baptist Convention.

55. Committee on Cuba to Díaz, Apr. 22, 1901 (in files of the Home Mission Board, Atlanta).

56. Díaz to Committee on Cuba, May 9, 1901; and Díaz to Tichenor, May 10, 1901 (in files of the Home Mission Board, Atlanta).

57. Copy of article from the *Havana Post*, Apr. 29, 1903 (in files of the Home Mission Board, Atlanta.)

58. Attorneys Conant and Wright to Home Mission Board, Jan. 5, 1907, in Minutes, Jan. 8, 1907.

59. Daniel to *Christian Index*, n.d., in *Christian Index* (Nov. 20, 1902), vol. 82, p. 4.

60. Cova, n.d., *Christian Index* (Sept. 29, 1904), vol. 84, p. 4.

61. C.E.W. Dobbs, "The Cuban Baptists in Convention," *Christian Index* (Feb. 29, 1912), vol. 92, p. 5.

62. Cova, n.d., *Christian Index* (Sept. 29, 1904), vol. 84, p. 4.

63. A. Pereira Alves, *Prominentes Evangélicos de Cuba* (El Paso: The Baptist Spanish Publishing House, 1936), pp. 13, 22–30, 64, 106–111; B. D. Gray, *A Trip to Cuba* (Atlanta, 1904), p. 5. (A pamphlet in the files of the Home Mission Board, Atlanta); and Una Roberts Lawrence, *Missionaries of the Home Mission Board* (Atlanta: Home Mission Board, 1936), p. 13.

64. Louie D. Newton, *Amazing Grace, the Life of M. N. McCall, Missionary to Cuba* (Atlanta: Home Mission Board, 1948), p. 88; Minutes, Dec. 5, 1905, Apr. 29, 1907, June 20, 1907; A. López Muñoz, *Apóstol Bautista en La Perla Antillana* (Havana: Editorial Federación, 1945), p. 66; and Una Roberts Lawrence, *Cuba for Christ* (Atlanta: Home Mission Board, 1926), pp. 283–284.

65. P. J. Franqui, "Trinidad, Cuba," *Our Home Field* (March 1907), vol. 18, p. 16.

66. C. D. Daniel, "Church Buildings for Cuba," *Christian Index* (July 21, 1904), vol. 84, p. 2.

67. Daniel, "Church Buildings for Cuba," p. 2.

68. Minutes, Mar. 14, 1904, May 19, 1904, Nov. 1, 1904, Feb. 17, 1905, Sept. 14, 1909; M. N. McCall, "Dedication of Colon Chapel," *Christian Index* (June 20, 1907), vol. 87, p. 5; *Annual*, 1908, pp. 214, 217; and McCall, "Progress in Cuba," *Our Home Field* (September 1911), vol. 22, p. 28.

69. Victor I. Masters, "Baptist Missions in Cuba," *Christian Index* (June 25, 1914), vol. 94, pp. 9–10.

70. *Annual*, 1907, p. 186; and L. T. Mays, *Cuban-American College* (Atlanta, c. 1907), p. 1. (A pamphlet in the files of the Home Mission Board, Atlanta.) The Spanish term *colegio* which was used for this school is a bit confusing, and is not exactly the equivalent of the English "college."

71. *History of Southern Baptist Convention Missions in Cuba* (Birmingham, Ala., n.d.). (A pamphlet in the files of the Home Mission Board, Atlanta.)

72. M. N. McCall, "From Cuba," *Christian Index* (Oct. 25, 1906), vol. 86, p. 5; and M. N. McCall, *A Baptist Generation in Cuba* (Atlanta, Home Mission Board, 1942), p. 34.

73. Lawrence, *Missionaries of the Home Mission Board*, p. 18.

74. B. D. Gray, report on trip to Cuba, January and February, 1905, in Minutes, Feb. 17, 1905.

75. McCall, *A Baptist Generation in Cuba*, pp. 57, 62–63.

76. David Cole, "The Cuban Baptist Convention," *Our Home Field* (April 1913), vol. 24, p. 15.

77. *Annual*, 1916, p. 47; McCall, *A Baptist Generation in Cuba*, p. 69;

Victor I. Masters, *Christ for Cuba* (Atlanta, n.d.), (a pamphlet in the files of the Home Mission Board, Atlanta); *Annual* (1916) p. 44; and McCall, "Hopefulness of the Cuban Outlook," *The Home Field* (October 1916), vol. 27, pp. 28–29.

78. McCall, *A Baptist Generation in Cuba*, p. 70; J. Milton Greene, "Fifteen Years in Cuba," *Missionary Review of the World* (March 1915), vol. 38, p. 181; and "By-Products of Christian Missions in Cuba," *Missionary Review of the World* (January 1912), vol. 35, p. 66.

6 | United States Conquest of the Mexican Market as Seen by British Officials, 1895-1905

Wilford H. Lane

Mexico exercised a magnetic attraction upon the English mind as early as the sixteenth-century voyages of John Hawkins and Francis Drake. The Hapsburg monarchs jealously guarded New Spain as their most prized possession in the New World, but British merchants and seamen found ways to break into its coveted trade.[1] These colonial contacts set the stage for an active commercial relationship between England and the new nation of Mexico following the overthrow of Spanish power. By 1824 Great Britain enjoyed a position of preeminence in industrial output, shipping facilities, and capital reserve. She developed governmental mail brigs and private packet lines, which touched at Tampico and Veracruz as well as other ports throughout the Caribbean. These advantages gave Great Britain a decided lead in trade with Mexico as well as with other nations of Latin America.[2]

At the time the United States gained its independence from Great Britain, it had already established a few commercial contacts with New Spain. As the young republic acquired Louisiana and Florida, it sought to increase its trade to the south. When Joel R. Poinsett was sent as minister to Mexico in 1825, he found that Great Britain occupied a dominant position in Mexican commerce and politics.[3] This situation changed but little in the following decades. Although United States merchant vessels improved greatly and often outclassed those of Britain, the long-established British financial interests gave that country the edge in Mexican trade. Moreover, the United States, still in the initial stages of her industrial development, remained dependent upon London for loans and upon other British cities for many products.[4]

By the middle of the nineteenth century, the United States had taken a series of important steps that strengthened its economic position. The annexation of Texas and the territory acquired by the treaty of Guadalupe Hidalgo pushed the borders of the "Yankee" republic closer to the Mexican capital. The discovery of gold in California sharpened the interests of United States businessmen in the prospects for a canal through Panama, Nicaragua, or the Isthmus of Tehuantepec. In 1850, Great Britain and the United States signed the Clayton-Bulwer Treaty by which each power agreed that any canal to be constructed should be neutral. Although this frustrated the dreams of those who wanted a canal dominated by the United States, it was actually a significant achievement for the young nation, in that Great Britain negotiated with it for the first time on a basis of equality.[5] The significance of this is even more apparent when one realizes that the British continued to enjoy a decided lead in the commerce of Middle America until after 1865. In 1871, the United States supplied less than one-sixth of Mexico's imports and purchased less than one-third of her exports.[6] The Civil War in the United States, however, was followed by a rapid expansion of industry and internal transportation. These changes, linked with the cooperation of a major political figure in Mexico, facilitated the conquest of the Mexican market by the business interests of the United States.

In 1876, Porfirio Díaz seized power in Mexico and retained almost total control of the nation's affairs until 1910. Surrounded by the *científicos*, President Díaz worked for order and economic progress, evoking highest praise from financial and political leaders throughout the world. The relationship between this Mexican strong man and the United States business interests is well known. His dictatorship brought stability to Mexico, and land companies and mining enterprises joined railroads and banking houses in investing vast sums there. By the early years of the twentieth century there was in Mexico a growing resentment against the Yankee capitalists because of their vast holdings.[7]

In commerce, too, rapid growth took place during the Díaz era. The greatest advances came in the decade of the 1880's, when both imports and exports almost doubled,[8] and in this same period the United States gained the lead over Great Britain in the Mexican trade.[9] Some of the reasons for the conquest of the Mexican market by the United States are quite obvious; for example, the geographic proximity of the two countries and the completion of railroad links between them. British officials in Mexico, however, sought for additional explanations for their nation's commercial losses. From 1895 to

1905, they made detailed studies of Mexican business trends, prepared statistical information, and attempted to interpret contributory factors. Through a study of these British reports, one can gain a new insight into the declining position of Great Britain in the Mexican market and, perhaps, a better understanding of the reasons for dominance of the United States.

In 1895, British officials were interested in the nature of goods purchased by the Mexicans, and therefore prepared a list of items which made up the bulk of the trade.

TABLE 1

PRINCIPAL ITEMS OF MEXICAN IMPORT (1895) [10]

	Source	
Item	*Great Britain* %	*United States* %
Textiles:		
Cottons	60	25
Linen	60	....
Woolens	25	10
Coal and coke	40–50	50
Iron and steel	30	55
Machinery	15–20	50–60
Chemical products	0–5	50
Paper products	0–2	30
Groceries and provisions	0–1	70
Arms and explosives	0–1	60
Copper, brass, spelter (zinc)	0–5	60–80
Wood	0–1	60–70
Petroleum	......	100
Leather	0–1	35
Carriages	......	80
Other articles	5	60

As can be seen from table 1, textile imports were dominated by the British in 1895, but the United States did offer some competition in cottons and woolens. Lionel Carden, British Consul in Mexico City, observed, however, that Mexico was rapidly developing a domestic cotton manufacturing industry, having imported 22,500,000 pounds

of ginned cotton from the United States in 1895. The adverse effect
of this on British trade was made even clearer by the statistics issued
by the Board of Trade, which showed that the importation of cotton
goods by Mexico from England in 1894 had been twenty percent
under the average for the previous ten years. This was not the whole
picture, however, for the cash value of the cotton goods imported
in 1894 had been forty-five percent higher than the ten-year average.[11]

In 1895, Mexico imported approximately 190,000 tons of coal and
95,000 tons of coke, the purchases being about evenly divided between the United States and Great Britain.[12] There was a reduction
in the importation of rails and railway equipment after the completion of the Mexican railroads, but the total importation of iron and
steel for 1895 was actually above that of the previous year. Though
the British enjoyed a sizable share of total sales of these products, the
norteamericanos had already won a decided edge.[13]

Machinery purchased abroad by Mexicans in 1895 was valued at
£823,000, an eighteen percent increase over that bought in 1894.
Here, too, the United States was in the lead, especially in mining
and agricultural machinery.[14] The United States also enjoyed an important advantage as a supplier of chemicals and paper products.[15]
Americans nearly monopolized the carriage sales because their products were light and especially suited for bad roads and country work.
All petroleum used in Mexico came from the United States, imported
in crude form and refined by the Waters Pierce Oil Company.[16]
Mexican oil deposits remained virtually untouched until 1901 when
the California oilman Edward L. Doheny began drilling operations
in the region.[17]

By September 1896, Lionel Carden reported that British trade in
Mexico was in a deplorable state. He felt that this was due largely to
the lack of British mercantile houses in the country, many of which
had been withdrawn during the period of Maximilian's empire. Carden indicated that Mexican trade had become more sophisticated,
that native manufactures were supplanting foreign goods in important areas, that the profit margin for importers was smaller than
in the past, and that competition was keener. The consul also believed that new mercantile houses were needed to create new markets for British goods. He stressed that they would need to be retail
houses, or at least retail-wholesale establishments that would cater to
the Mexican lower classes who, by reason of their large numbers,

were potentially important customers. American and German manufacturers were aware of this situation, and their brands of hardware and cutlery, for example, were preferred to the British because of their superior finish, even though they were less durable. Carden stated bluntly that the British could compete in the Mexican market only if they would take lessons from their rivals and pay more attention to the preferences of the Mexican customers.[18]

Two years later (1898) F. W. Stronge, Secretary of the British Legation in the Mexican capital, repeated the warning to British manufacturers. Unlike Carden, he stressed the fact that in Mexico there was a growing class of people who demanded superior goods and that Great Britain was not getting its share of the increased sales resulting from that demand. He pointed out that the few of his countrymen in Mexico who were active in foreign trade had little or no capital of their own and acted only as agents for British firms. Most of these individuals were inferior to their predecessors, and they were not so well versed in the language and knowledge of the country as their competitors. In this instance the British manufacturer was much to blame, because too often the agent was placed in the position, not of trying to please his Mexican customers, but of finding an outlet for surplus British goods that were ill-suited to the market. Secretary Stronge warned that trade in Mexico was no longer insignificant and that competition was keen. Already some branches of that trade were monopolized by Germany and the United States, and both were serious rivals for those areas of trade still in British hands. German and United States firms were also more actively pushing their businesses.[19]

One factor in particular prevented the British from increasing their sales in Mexico appreciably during the period under consideration. During the 1870's textiles had formed almost fifty percent of the total value of Mexican purchases abroad, and Great Britain had been the principal supplier. By the 1890's, however, textile products formed only seventeen percent of Mexico's total imports.[20]

Secretary Stronge pointed out that British trade in Mexico could be expanded only by competent agents with some freedom of operation. Much business was done in Mexico on the basis of friendship, and Mexican buyers would not assume unnecessary risks. There was a need for British companies to give prompt attention to orders and to exercise care in packing and shipping. He stressed the fact that United States firms were less reluctant in extending credit in order to get new business than were British houses. Stronge recommended that machinery for the Mexican market be light and comparatively cheap because of the expense and difficulty of transportation. He also pointed out that with railroad connections to Mexico, the United States producers were able to give quick deliveries.[21]

Great Britain was the traditional source of most of Mexico's iron and steel. By 1898, however, manufacturers of mining and smelting machinery from the United States formed a company and opened a warehouse to meet the demands of the Mexican market. United States firms also furnished most of Mexico's steam engines by that time, and with the establishment of a large Singer office in Mexico City the Yankees gained the upper hand in the sewing machine trade.[22] By the beginning of the twentieth century they also dominated the supply of agricultural machinery, largely due to the fact that broken parts could be more easily replaced. The British threshing machine was recognized as being superior to United States models in finish and adjustment, and it gave better service. The difficulty in obtaining parts for the British machines, however, caused orders to go to the United States.[23]

By 1898 the United States supplied sixty-five percent of the shoes and boots imported by Mexico.[24] Over the following six years the lead increased. British agents asserted that this was the result of United States companies providing the cheapest shoes of the commonest quality and using lasts that conformed to the feet of the

TABLE 2

GROWTH OF MEXICAN IMPORTS (1896–1905)[27]

Year	Value (£ millions)	Great Britain %	United States %
1896	9.4	17	53
1897	7.8	19	49
1898	9.1	18	49
1899	11.2	19	49
1900	13.1	17	52
1901	12.5	15	56
1902	14.5	13	58
1903	15.2	14	53
1904	15.7	13	54
1905	17.8	12	56

Mexican people. In 1905 the British agent in Veracruz warned British shoe manufacturers of the threat to their business because of growing competition from the United States.[25]

According to representatives in Mexico, British merchants were frequently remiss in their observance of tariff requirements and other regulations. The failure of shippers to determine the proper classification of articles on bills of lading and consular invoices caused the Mexican consignee to pay costly fines and was a source of great annoyance. Consuls urged British merchants to use care in following the shipping instructions of their Mexican customers, since their directions were designed to reduce expenses either in duties or freight. Failure in this matter often caused goods to be kept on hand or sold at a loss that could not be regained from the shipper. The indifference of British merchants to these matters, as well as long delays in filling orders, frequently caused large contracts to be placed in the United States rather than in Great Britain.[26] A summary of the decline of British trade with Mexico from 1896 to 1905 is given in table 2.

TABLE 3
PRINCIPAL ITEMS OF MEXICAN EXPORT (1895)[28]

	Destination	
	Great Britain	United States
Item	%	%
Silver: coin	20	80
ore	25	75
bullion	20	80
base bullion (argentiferous lead)	----	95–100
Gold	19	62
Copper	95–100	----
Dyewoods	50	10
Cabinet woods	67	33
Chicle	----	100
Coffee	4–5	90
Sisal hemp	----	90
Shortleaf agave	20	60
Hides, fruits, vanilla, marble & cattle	----	80

Possibly one of the most important reasons for the growth of United States markets in Mexico at the turn of the twentieth century was the simple fact that the United States was Mexico's best customer. As early as 1895, the growing industrial nation to the north absorbed three-quarters of Mexico's exports. This was largely due to the nature of the Mexican products which had a much higher demand in the United States. (See Table 3.)

In 1895, Great Britain ranked as the second-best customer even though she took only some fifteen percent of Mexico's total exports. One-fourth of these consisted of Mexican silver dollars,[29] which were undoubtedly sent to British trade areas in Asia and Europe. The United States overshadowed Great Britain as a market for Mexico's silver ore and bullion, base bullion, and gold.[30]

With the exception of copper, dyewoods, and cabinet woods, the United States was the largest consumer of Mexican products, and in the case of chicle the Americans were the exclusive buyers. Mexico sold most of her coffee and sisal hemp to the United States, because the British had little use for either. The bulk of Mexican hides, fruits, vanilla, marble, and cattle were shipped to the United States. Cattle exports to that nation were seventy-five percent larger in 1895 than they had been the previous year, as Texas stockmen sought to replenish herds that had been decimated by two years of drought. About £35,000 worth of shortleaf agave, the fibers of which were used in cheap scrubbing brushes, went to the United States and a much smaller quantity to England.[31]

TABLE 4
GROWTH OF MEXICAN EXPORTS (1895–1905)[32]

Year	Value (£ millions)	Great Britain %	United States %
1896	11.7	14	74
1897	12.9	14	77
1898	13.9	10	73
1899	14.1	7	78
1900	16.9	11	76
1901	14.9	8	80
1902	16.5	11	77
1903	18.6	12	72
1904	19.7	13	72
1905	20.8	8	73

In the decade following 1895, the nature of Mexico's production changed very little. There was, however, a steady increase in the volume of her sales, with exports ranging from £2,000,000 to £5,-000,000 higher than imports each year. The United States continued to buy the greater share of these exports, as seen in table 4.

The total foreign trade of Mexico at the turn of the century was clearly dominated by the United States. This is illustrated in table 5.

TABLE 5

MEXICO'S TOTAL FOREIGN TRADE (1896–1905)

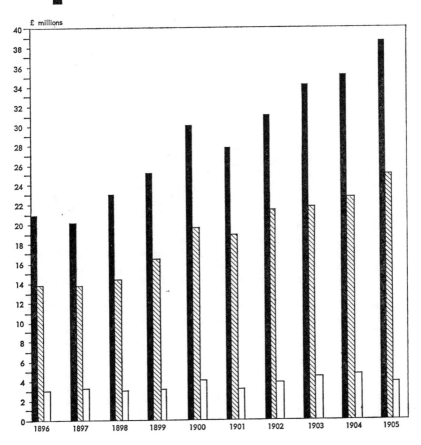

In 1905, the clerk of His Majesty's legation in Mexico summarized the situation in the following terms:

> In the early part of the last century the whole commerce was practically controlled by British merchants and bankers, and even as late as the early seventies the advance of any undertaking was in great measure due to British enterprise. Since the construction of the railways in 1875–88 the supremacy in all enterprises has passed into American hands.[38]

Certainly the construction of the railroads provided a distinct advantage for the business interests of the United States that wished to penetrate the Mexican market. The rail link, however, was only one factor in this complex mosaic of international trade. Behind it lay the broader factors of the growing American industrial complex, capable of supplying Mexican demands in sufficient volume. Enterprising Yankee businessmen, eager to develop these markets, found little competition from their complacent British counterparts. Probably the most significant factor of all in the United States conquest of the Mexican market, however, was that Mexican products found an almost insatiable demand in the United States, thus producing a mutual trade to the benefit of both parties.

Notes

1. Herbert E. Bolton and Thomas M. Marshall, *The Colonization of North America, 1492–1783* (New York: The Macmillan Company, 1920), pp. 107, 132–133, 152–153, 206–208.

2. Robert G. Albion, "British Shipping in Latin America, 1806–1914," *The Journal of Economic History*, (Fall, 1951), vol. 2, pp. 363–365.

3. J. Fred Rippy, *Joel R. Poinsett, Versatile American* (Durham, N.C.: Duke University Press, 1935), pp. 107–117.

4. Albion, "British Shipping," pp. 361–363.

5. Mary W. Williams, *Anglo-American Isthmian Diplomacy, 1815–1915* (Washington: American Historical Association, 1916), p. 92; and Thomas A. Bailey, *A Diplomatic History of the American People*, 3d ed. (New York: F.S. Crofts & Co., 1946), pp. 292–293. Bailey believes that in view of the United States' position as a second-rate power in 1850, the Clayton-Bulwer Treaty fell just short of an American diplomatic victory.

6. U.S. Congress, House, *Annual Report on the Commercial Relations between The United States and Foreign Countries*, House Executive Document no. 160, 42d Cong., 3d sess. (1871–1872), pp. 672–673.

7. Henry B. Parkes, *A History of Mexico* (Boston: Houghton Mifflin Company, 1950), pp. 308–310; and Wigberto Jiménez Moreno, José Miranda, and María Teresa Fernández, *Compendio de História de México* (México, Editorial E.C.L.A.L.S.A., 1966), pp. 443–444.

8. See tables in text for trade increases.

9. U.S. Bureau of Foreign Commerce, *Commercial Relations of the United States with Foreign Countries* (Washington, D.C.: Government Printing Office, 1880 and 1881), p. 64.

10. Great Britain, *Sessional Papers* (Commons), Edgar L. Erickson, ed., "Diplomatic and Consular Reports on Trade and Finance" (September 1896), Annual Series, vol. 92 (1897), no. 1827, pp. 184–190 (hereinafter cited as Erickson, *BSP*, Con. Reports, AS).

11. Ibid., pp. 185–186.

12. Ibid., p. 184.

13. Ibid., p. 187.

14. Ibid., p. 188.

15. Ibid., p. 188–189.

16. Ibid., p. 189–190.

17. Parker T. Moon, *Imperialism and World Politics* (New York: The Macmillan Company, 1927), p. 438. There was no competition in oil drilling from the British until 1905, when a certain Mr. Pearson became a vigorous rival.

18. Erickson, *BSP*, Con. Reports (September 1896), AS, vol. 92 (1897), no. 1827, pp. 190–191.

19. Erickson, *BSP*, Con. Reports (November 1898), Miscellaneous Series, vol. 97 (1899), no. 486, pp. 631–632 (hereinafter cited as Erickson, *BSP*, Con Reports, MS).

20. Erickson, *BSP*, Con. Reports (August 1898), AS, vol. 101 (1899), no. 2184, p. 16.

21. Erickson, *BSP*, Con. Reports (November 1898), MS, vol. 97 (1899), no. 486, pp. 633–634.

22. Erickson, *BSP*, Con. Reports (July 1899), AS, vol. 101 (1899), no. 2336, pp. 70–73.

23. Great Britain, *Foreign Office* (1901), Diplomatic and Consular Reports (December 1900), Annual Series, no. 2546, pp. 20–21 (hereinafter cited as Great Britain, *FO*, Con. Reports, AS).

24. Erickson, *BSP*, Con. Reports (July 1899), AS, vol. 101 (1899), no. 2336, pp. 70–73.

25. Great Britain, *FO* (1906), Con. Reports (July 1905), AS, no. 3503, pp. 6–7.

26. Great Britain, *FO* (1901), Con. Reports (December 1900), AS, no. 2546, pp. 18–20.

27. Erickson, *BSP*, Con. Reports (1897, 1898, 1899 and 1900), AS, vols. 92, 97, 101, and 95, nos. 1827, 1985, 2336, and 2527; and Great Britain, *FO*, Con. Reports, (1901, 1903, 1904, 1905, and 1907), AS, nos. 2546, 2693, 2925, 3112, 3332, 3429, and 3888.

28. Erickson, *BSP*, Con. Reports (September 1896), AS, vol. 92 (1897), no. 1827, pp. 190–195.

29. Ibid., pp. 191–192. The majority of exports to the United States were for consumption in that country, but £1,300,000 worth of Mexican silver dollars consigned to the United States were destined to be shipped to China and Europe. These silver dollars were sent by way of San

Francisco and New York, which were the most direct routes to their ultimate destinations. They should, therefore, be properly considered as transit trade.

30. Ibid., pp. 192–193.

31. Ibid., pp. 193–195.

32. Erickson, *BSP*, Con. Reports (Various months), AS, vols. 92, 95, 97, 101, nos. 1827, 1985, 2336, and 2527; and Great Britain, *FO*, Con. Reports (1901, 1903, 1904, 1905, and 1907), nos. 2546, 2693, 2925, 3112, 3332, 3429, and 3888.

33. Great Britain, *FO* (1905) Con. Reports, (July 1901), AS, no. 3332, p. 23.

7 | Albert Edward Bishop and the Establishment of the Central American Mission in Guatemala, 1899-1922

Wilkins B. Winn

Justo Rufino Barrios was elected president of Guatemala in 1873, and he immediately launched a program of liberal reforms, highlighted by the Constitution of 1879. This document provided for extensive individual guarantees, including complete freedom of religion. Barrios actively encouraged Protestants to establish missions in his country, hoping that they would act as a counterforce to clerical interference in political affairs. As might be expected, church groups in the United States saw this as a golden opportunity, and as early as 1882 the Presbyterian Board of Foreign Missions responded to an invitation of President Barrios by sending John C. Hill to begin the missionary work in Guatemala. The favorable liberal climate continued after the death of Barrios in 1885, and other denominations from the United States followed the Presbyterians.[1] The story of this Protestant missionary activity is a part of the broader picture of a growing United States penetration into Middle America. That entire process can be better understood through an examination of the career of Albert Edward Bishop who engaged in missionary activities for over a quarter-century.

The Central American Mission was established in 1890 at Dallas, Texas; its primary aim was the spread of Bible teachings throughout Middle America. In 1896, Albert Edward Bishop, a thirty-five-year-old former merchant from Abilene, Kansas, accepted an invitation from the organization to become a missionary to Honduras. For three years the young preacher successfully carried out this assignment, but in 1899 he moved to Guatemala because the opportunities there seemed greater.[2] After arriving in Guatemala City, he and his wife began intensive evangelistic work, conducting street meetings and making house-to-house visitations. Bishop felt that street meetings were the most effective way to reach the potential converts. He rented a building in a strategic location at the junction of five streets; later it was to be known as the Cinco Calles Church. On good market days about ten thousand people, mostly Indians, passed the point and Bishop took full advantage of the location. He later commented on the initial phase of his efforts: "We had meetings seven nights a week. For 150 succeeding nights I did not fail once in being there." [3]

Another means of establishing initial contacts was through the use of religious literature. At the annual fair of Guatemala City in August 1899, Bishop distributed thousands of tracts. His personal contacts, however, proved even more successful. When his preaching to a Quiché Indian woman, who had a fruit stand on a principal street, resulted in her conversion, Bishop stated: "Surely the Lord is beginning to answer our prayers for the poor Indians. To me it seems He must have a purpose towards the two hundred eighty thousand Quiché Indians in the conversion of this woman." [4] Shortly thereafter sixteen other Indians accepted Protestantism as a result of his using this new convert as his interpreter. These efforts led to the establishment of a small congregation, which by April 1, 1900 consisted of thirty baptized believers. Many others had by that time indicated an interest in the teachings but had not been baptized.

The arrival of several additional missionaries by 1900 permitted Bishop to return to the United States for a furlough, and J. G. Cassel assumed control of the work in his absence. Bishop returned in 1902, accompanied by five new missionaries. These workers, however, did not remain in Guatemala City, but opened new centers in the provinces.[5] In the capital city the returning evangelist renewed his busy schedule, describing his activities in the following terms:

> The meetings continue every night as before, the believers being unwilling to abandon a single night. One night in the week we have a believers' prayer meeting; one night lessons from the Old Testament; another night one of the believers has charge of the meeting, and the other four evenings of the week are given to straight gospel preaching. On Sunday we have a service for the children; another for the believers in which our Lord is remembered in the breaking of bread, and where doctrinal truths are presented for the establishment of the believers. On Saturday afternoon all of the missionaries meet for conference and prayer.[6]

He emphasized the importance of Bible study on Thursday nights, when the periods were dedicated to doctrinal teaching, especially those in the Epistles to the Romans and Galatians.[7] Visitation programs and the distribution of literature also continued as a basic part of his missionary effort. Two Guatemalan converts distributed almost five thousand Gospels and tracts during the annual fair of 1909.[8] By 1918 Bishop and his fellow workers were conducting weekly thirty meetings of various types. Among these were special services for the Negro workers in the railroad yards and other mass evangelistic efforts.[9]

In addition to purely religious activities, the Central American Mission undertook an educational program, beginning with a day school for the children of converts. Some of the support came from contributions by members of the Cinco Calles Church. The first teacher was a Guatemalan convert who had taught in public schools.[10] In 1915, Miss Estelle Zimmerman and Miss A. Fern Houser arrived to assume direction of the day school. They established a mission-supported orphanage which housed 45 girls and boys by 1922. By that time there were 115 children in the school. These facilities provided employment for 6 Guatemalan girls, and afforded the missionaries an opportunity to reach the parents of many of the students.[11]

The principal building of the Mission was heavily damaged by earthquakes in 1917 and 1918, and an improved structure replaced the original one. The new auditorium accommodated five hundred people, with provision for overflow crowds in a patio and annex. That this facility served many purposes can be seen from a statement by Bishop in 1919:

> On the second floor there are eight dormitories and the office, where the correspondence of the Mission and the duplicating of many Bible lessons and all clerical work is taken care of. There is a commodious sitting room, where believers can come for conference and where the weekly meetings of the Sunday School teachers are held, also dental parlors where native pastors and evangelists may have their dental work done at cost of material and where many of the Lord's poor receive treatment gratis. In an annex back of the building there are eleven apartments used for Sunday School classes, dormitories for native believers who come in from out-stations as well as rooms for the caretaker and his family.[12]

With these new facilities and the continued efforts of Bishop and his staff, the membership and attendance of the Cinco Calles Church steadily increased. The missionary was afraid, however, that some members might not fully understand the fundamental teachings and precepts of the faith that they professed. Converts were tested by a period of waiting before their baptism in order to ascertain the reality of their conversion. Bishop was especially concerned over the problem of common-law marriages and often postponed baptisms until legal marriages were performed.[13] After baptizing twenty-four people on a trip to the coast in 1905 the evangelist lamented, ". . . there are nearly as many more who give evidence of saving faith, but who are not in condition as yet to be baptized. A number of them are living together as man and wife, who have not been able to legalize their union so far." [14] This problem persisted, for in 1912 Miss Houser commented, "few of the common and lower classes are married legally." [15]

The caution exercised in baptism did not prevent some converts from "falling away," and thus suffering dismissal from the congregation. Bishop expressed the wish that all who were received into fellowship might be like some who had remained faithful for years, but lamented that ". . . ofttimes we have to mourn the contrary, and the dismissal of some who return after a shorter or longer time to their former corrupt manner of life, is not, we are sorry to say, infrequent." [16] Many of the converts, however, remained faithful, manifesting changes in their actions and attitudes. One example was Manuel Marroquín, a criminal and a drunkard, whose conduct underwent a complete change after his conversion.[17] Another, Mariano Gonzales, favorably impressed officials of the electric light company for which he worked. They indicated that ". . . previous to his conversion [Gonzales] was as irresponsible as any man in their employ, but . . . after his conversion they had no man so faithful." [18]

Native members contributed a portion of their income to support the work of the Cinco Calles Church. In the first quarter of 1905 offerings in that church amounted to more than $1,400 in Guatemalan money.[19] A financial report for the church that ended a six-month period on December 31, 1921 revealed the income from gifts as $48,276.00.[20] Bishop officiated as pastor of this congregation and was aided by a Guatemalan assistant pastor. A system of elders, both ruling and teaching, completed the basic ecclesiastical leadership. Under this arrangement the Cinco Calles Church became the parent congregation of the Central American Mission churches of Guatemala. Its influence spread over much of that republic. By 1912, work was carried on in twelve outstations, manned by national workers from the capital city. In 1921, the Cinco Calles Church included nine

national workers in its budget and financially aided infant and strug-
gling churches throughout the nation.[21]

Albert Bishop often made evangelistic trips into every section of
Guatemala, even during the rainy season, when virtually all other
travel ceased.[22] F. G. Toms accompanied him in 1903 on a six-week
trip to the western part of the Republic. They spent five days at
San Martín and baptized five persons. Continuing on to Tecpán,
they strengthened the faith of a group of believers who had "faltered
in their constancy." At Santo Tomás the ministers visited an independent missionary who was working among the Quiché Indians.
When they reached Totonicapán, a city of forty thousand inhabitants, Bishop and Toms learned that some of the residents were
interested in the establishment of a Protestant mission in their community. After stopping briefly at Quezaltenango, the travelers turned
northwest to San Marcos, where for eleven days they aided the mission efforts of Misses Anna R. Alloway and Fannie C. Buck. Bishop
and Toms instructed the believers in the afternoons and preached at
night. Having baptized fifteen converts in San Marcos, they returned
to Guatemala City. In the following years Bishop continued to
travel, supervising the work in various outstations and congregations
as well as preaching. In 1910, he reported that he had traveled about
one thousand miles.[23]

The number of converts steadily increased in the territory in
which Bishop labored. In May 1917, the mission leader stated:

> God, in His providence, has given me as a special field of labor, 6 of
> the 18 provinces of Guatemala. In two other provinces we share
> equally with another mission. In the 6 not another mission is at work.
> In this territory, a stretch 200 x 100 miles, we have our 15 native
> workers located at advantageous centers.[24]

This area constituted more than one-third of the total area of Guatemala. By 1921, there were twenty-eight national workers who attempted to minister to the 567,600 persons in this territory.[25]

The basic method of carrying teaching into the countryside was
the establishment of outstations related to the Guatemala City center.
The size of these rural congregations varied from 60 to 125 members.
El Baúl in eastern Guatemala, near Santa Lucía, was an example of a
rural outstation. This was a *finca* of about seventy-five hundred acres;
it had four hundred tenant houses, and extensive coffee and sugar
refining establishments. In 1919 the church at El Baul consisted of

200 members, many of whom were Indians who spoke only the Cakchiquel tongue.[26]

By 1921 the Guatemala mission had increased to 145 congregations with a total of 2,850 believers, who were engaged in some 223 services weekly. The number of baptisms also steadily increased; over 100 were reported in July and August of that year.[27] Although these figures indicated growth, Bishop felt that much work remained to be done. In January, 1921 he observed that ". . . a late estimate states that as yet only 7 of each 100 of the population of Guatemala have been evangelized." [28] He was determined to leave no town or village "unworked." He realized, however, that he could not do the job alone.

Bishop believed that the evangelization of Guatemala was to be achieved by the work of well-trained native converts under the direction of missionaries. He devoted his best efforts to the preparation and direction of Guatemalan workers as well as to preaching. He stated in 1910: "God is giving us many faithful workers among our converts and my foremost work since the beginning, 14 years ago, has been to train them in the scriptures of truth." [29] These efforts produced rewarding results, for within a few years the native workers were carrying out roles that were ". . . indispensable to the evangelization of Guatemala." [30] Their effectiveness was largely due to the fact that they came from many different social backgrounds, including "the Indian with his tribal garb and the bare-foot halfbreed." [31]

From time to time the native workers met for conferences, in which they engaged in Bible studies and discussed methods to improve their evangelistic and pastoral effectiveness. Bishop took advantage of the Catholic celebration of Holy Week to conduct an annual workers' and believers' conference in the capital city. In April 1916, the mission leader remarked: "We plan Bible Study Conference here for 20th–25th, last week of Lent when all the world in Guatemala are occupied, even the street cars, as well as all the business being suspended." [32] This arrangement proved quite satisfactory, for during the five-day conference of 1919 every native assistant except one attended.[33] Various problems, both administrative and spiritual, were solved at these meetings.[34]

Although the conferences served to train workers, Bishop recognized the need for a central Bible institute. In 1920 he wrote that "present conditions make urgent the establishment of a practical Bible School in this metropolis for the training of native workers in the fundamentals." [35] These plans for a Central American Bible Institute, however, did not materialize until the next decade.

Despite the liberal policy of the Guatemalan government toward Protestant activities, the work of the Central American Mission faced rather stringent opposition from the Roman Catholic Church. In the very first year of his activities in Guatemala, Bishop complained that the priests would often "stir things up," thus turning prospective members against the missionaries.[36] A special "Prayer to our Lady of Guadalupe Against the Evangelist Sect," was circulated by the Archbishop of Santiago de Guatemala. It emphasized that Roman Catholicism was the true religion, which all of Latin America professed, and that the "wolfish sect" which had penetrated into the region was dressed in lamb's skin and covered its heretical doctrines with a false religiousness and fictitious piety. The prayer petitioned:

> Do not permit your parish to be infected with venomous heresy. . . .
> Thou all powerful Virgin, hast smashed with the sole of your Immaculate foot every heresy; smash now, we pray it of you fervently, the perfidious imposter and poisonous evangelism.[37]

The Archbishop granted one hundred days indulgence to the faithful Catholics who repented of their sins and recited this prayer with devotion. On the other hand, individuals who attended Protestant services faced the threat of excommunication.

Various means were used to intimidate Protestant missionaries and to discredit their work. As a group of Catholics paraded in the streets of Zacapa, Guatemala, a priest sprinkled holy water in front of the Protestant mission before the procession was allowed to continue. On another occasion demonstrators tore up an effigy of Judas in front of the mission in Guatemala City.[38] In 1921 a visiting priest told the people at the village of La Democracia that he would not return unless all Protestant believers were forced to leave. Following this, the people of the town threatened the Protestant converts, forcing them either to abandon their meetings or to hold them in the mountains.[39] Municipal authorities sided with the priests instead of trying to prevent these attacks.[40]

At times the missionaries were threatened with physical violence to both property and person. More often, however, their opponents used subtler methods, such as blocking their attempts to secure adequate housing for living quarters and meetings. After being denied the use of a building in Antigua, Bishop lamented:

> A good Catholic may rent his building for a low down saloon or gambling den without incurring any opposition from the priest, but the one who permits his house to be used for the proclamation of the Blessed Gospel, brings upon himself quickly, curses, excommunication, and persecution.[41]

Possibly the most damaging charge levied against the Protestants was that they were engaged in subversive political activity. As early as 1896 a French Catholic missionary to Costa Rica issued a circular to all the Catholics of that nation, warning them against the Protestant sect called "The Undenominationals." Missionaries of this organization, he charged, were "spiritual filibusters," who should be ejected from the country.[42] The same attack was made in Guatemala the following year, and convinced many people that the Protestants had been "sent by the Queen of England" or were engaged in commercial ventures.[43] One Protestant worker, H. C. Dillon, observed that the Guatemalans found it difficult to realize that the missionaries were there solely for religious purposes.[44] Political factions within Guatemala attempted to capitalize on the relationship between the party in power and the Protestant workers. In 1921 *El Unionista*, the newspaper of a proclerical political party, printed an article entitled "Democrats and Evangelists." This story charged that the missionaries were the vanguard of "the tribes of the north," who were engaged in the conquest of the country, and that they were supported by the Guatemalan Liberal Party.[45]

In the early days of his work Albert Bishop was often faced with acts of violence. In 1899 he had received permission from the governmental authorities to read and preach the Holy Scriptures on the streets of Guatemala City. He reported the following year, however, that ". . . on account of previous fanatical disturbances in our street meetings, our permission to preach on the streets was revoked under pretense of protection to us, and the avoidance of serious disturbances."[46] Mob demonstrations sometimes resulted in physical violence to persons and mission property. In 1899 mud and brickbats, among other things, were thrown through the open door of the meeting room. Following some arrests by the police, the more violent acts ceased.[47] In January of the following year, however, the attacks were renewed. One evening during a meeting on the porch of a building, Bishop was struck on the forehead, and the "blood flowed freely." [48]

The most serious attacks against the mission work took place in Guatemala City in 1905. On Good Friday of that year, as a large Catholic procession passed the mission building, a drunken man in the crowd threw a stone. Members of the procession began to yell: "The Masons are stoning the Lord." [49] The police accompanied the crowd into the mission building, and arrested several of the members, "beating them shamefully." [50] The next morning at ten o'clock, the customary time for destroying the images of Judas, Bishop was shocked as ". . . the rabble fell upon our old Mission, tore down the doors and almost destroyed the building, entered and literally demolished every article on the inside including our valuable new organ." [51] The mission leader also reported that some of the leaders of the attacks shouted "we have destroyed the Mission property and now we are going to destroy the native believers and the Missionaries, and put an end to this whole detestable work." [52] These threats were never carried out. In fact, when the United States authorities brought the matter to the attention of the Guatemalan government, it took immediate action, paying for the damaged property and establishing a guard to protect the mission and all of its workers. [53]

Guatemalan converts to Protestantism encountered many special problems in their private lives. Native Protestants suffered arrests, imprisonment, and conscription into the army because of their religious position. They also faced the threat of losing friends, wives, children, and jobs. [54] Children of converts were abused and persecuted in public schools, especially when they refused to participate in the Catholic worship taught there. This, of course, discouraged many children from accepting Protestantism, even when their parents had been baptized. It was this situation that helped Albert Bishop decide, in 1900, to establish the mission school. [55]

Some employers, especially the large landowners of the countryside, were very suspicious of Protestant influences among their workers. In 1908 J. G. Cassel described the reaction of one *hacendado* at San Marcos:

> I have . . . been forbidden to enter the plantation by the owner, who is an unreasonable Roman Catholic. He says the Indians without vices are not good, and since faith in the gospel of Christ saves them from drunkenness and other vices he claims the gospel is an enemy

of agriculture. The explanation of this strange position is that while the Indian is a hard drinker and follows the R. C. religious customs, he needs more money continually and thus becomes hopelessly indebted to the plantation and is to all purposes and intents a slave; but when the power of the gospel gets hold of him he is not only freed from the slavery of sin and vice, but also seeks to free himself from the slavery of debt. Thus the plantation owners lose their dominion over him. This makes the men I refer to angry, claiming the gospel hurts his business.[56]

A. E. Bishop played a key role in all of the activities of the Central American Mission. Not only did he preach, teach, and supervise the activities of the national workers, he also kept financial records, issued regular circular and pastoral letters, and wrote tracts and Bible lessons. He personally counseled the members of the various congregations and even translated important books into Spanish for his Guatemalan assistants. He welcomed new missionaries from the United States, assisted them in passing through the custom house, found homes for them, and gave them valuable training. His home in Guatemala City was, in his words, a "veritable hotel," with missionaries coming and going all the time.[57] These pressing duties, however, did not prevent Bishop from a daily devotional reading of the Bible.[58]

In June 1920, Bishop and his wife went to Escuintla for a rest. During the four days there, however, he ". . . held three meetings, wrote a copy for circular letter to the Native Pastors, and copy for two [Sunday School] Lessons, besides different private interviews with believers touching grievances." [59] The missionary leader had not had a vacation for nine years, and he had worked seven days a week during much of that time.[60] The Council for the Central American Mission called upon Bishop to assist them in administrative decisions. He often toured through other nations of Central America in order to evaluate missionary activities. These increasing duties placed a heavy burden on the evangelist's physical strength. From time to time he suffered attacks of influenza; by 1921 he had developed a nervous condition. When his wife also became ill, Bishop decided that it was necessary for them to return to the United States for a rest. Even at that time he was very reluctant to leave the work, but knew that his strength would not permit further delay.[61] The Bishops left Guatemala City on June 23, 1922. Because of the severity of his illness, the missionary was unable to return to his assignment until 1926.

A. E. Bishop remained active in the Central American Mission for seventeen more years. The pioneer work which he carried out from 1899 to 1922, however, constituted his most fruitful contribution to the spread of Protestantism in Guatemala. Bishop also exercised a wide influence in the cultural, intellectual, and ethical spheres of the nation. He injected Protestant concepts through his preaching and teaching, as well as through the distribution of Bibles and other religious literature. He attacked illiteracy by establishing schools and adult Bible classes. By his teaching of systematic tithing and the Protestant concepts of thrift and economy, the native members of his church learned to apply new methods to their personal finances.

The career of Albert E. Bishop also influenced political developments in the nation in which he worked. The liberal reforms initiated by President Justo Rufino Barrios had made it possible for Protestants to enter Guatemala. Bishop and other missionaries, in turn, supported such liberal concepts as freedom of religion, speech, and press. They were also advocates of the separation of Church and State. Through these common interests, Protestant workers and political liberals mutually strengthened each other. Perhaps the most significant influences stemmed from the fact that the Protestant mission work brought a new element into the citizens of Guatemala. By 1922 almost three thousand individuals had accepted the Protestant faith as a result of the efforts of Albert E. Bishop and his associates, and though still a small minority, their number has continued to grow until the present day.

Notes

1. Alfred B. Thomas, *Latin America: A History* (New York: The Macmillan Company, 1956), pp. 602–603; and Adolph L. Blakeney, "The Origin and Growth of Protestantism in Guatemala, 1824–1950" (M.A. thesis, University of Alabama, 1956), pp. 54–59.

2. "Diary of A. E. Bishop, April 29, 1896 to January 28, 1898" (MS in possession of Miss Mary A. Bishop, Los Angeles, Calif.). See references throughout this diary; and A. E. Bishop, "History of the Entrance and Development of the Work of the Central American Mission in Honduras and Guatemala" (MS in the Archives of the Central American Mission, April, 1935, hereinafter cited as ACAM. When no initials are given, "Bishop" refers to A. E. Bishop.).

3. Bishop, "History," pp. 12–13.

4. Bishop, Sept. 30, 1899, *The Central American Bulletin* (October 1899), vol. 5, p. 10 (hereinafter cited as *C.A.B.*); Bishop, Aug. 18, 1899, *C.A.B.* (October 1899), vol. 5, p. 9; and Bishop, Oct. 20, 1899, *C.A.B.* (January 1900), vol. 6, p. 8. In instances such as this where no addressee is given, it is assumed that the letter is addressed either to the periodical or to someone who then turned it over to the periodical.

5. Bishop, "History," pp. 13–14.

6. Bishop, May 15, 1902, *C.A.B.* (July 1902), vol. 8, pp. 7–8.

7. Bishop, July 1, 1912, *C.A.B.* (July 1912), vol. 18, p. 7.

8. Bishop, Sept. 1, 1909, *C.A.B.* (October 1909), vol. 15, pp. 5–6.

9. Bishop, Apr. 30, 1918, *C.A.B.* (July 1918), vol. 24, p. 9; A. B. Treichler, Oct. 26, 1918, *C.A.B.* (January 1919), vol. 25, p. 7; and Bishop, April 1, 1913, *C.A.B.* (April, 1913), vol. 19, p. 7.

10. Bishop, Mar. 29, 1905, *C.A.B.* (April 1905), vol. 11, p. 14.

11. Miss A. Fern Houser, June 6, 1916, *C.A.B.* (July 1916), vol. 22, p. 15; and Miss B. Estelle Zimmerman, June 12, 1922, *C.A.B.* (July 1922), vol. 28, pp. 7–8. In her letter, Miss Houser stated: "Several of the unconverted parents will come to this meeting who are afraid to come to other meetings."

12. Bishop, Apr. 22, 1919, *C.A.B.* (May 1919), vol. 25, p. 5.

13. Bishop, Dec. 27, 1905, *C.A.B.* (January 1906), vol. 12, p. 13. Bishop commented ". . . a goodly number are awaiting baptism as soon as the marriage of some three couples can be arranged, who have already lived together—one of them as much as 18 years."

14. Bishop, Jan. 30, 1907, *C.A.B.* (April 1907), vol. 13, p. 7.

15. Houser, Feb. 19, 1912, *C.A.B.* (April 1912), vol. 18, p. 19. Her explanation was that it seemed "difficult to get the papers from the church."

16. Bishop, June 22, 1906, *C.A.B.* (July 1906), vol. 12, pp. 19–20.

17. A. E. Bishop, "The Transforming Power of the Gospel," *C.A.B.* (October 1906), vol. 12, p. 6. Bishop stated of Marroquín: "Although not over 30 years of age, he had paid the penalty in some measure for his multipled [*sic*] crimes, by 63 imprisonments in the jails of different towns throughout Guatemala. The wife who was repeatedly beaten in the drunken brawls, which occurred at least every Sunday, is now loved and caressed. The delicate little children who were more dead than alive, half starved and illy clad by an ungrateful father, that he might satisfy his hellish appetite for drink, are now well clothed and cared for by one of the most constant, faithful and attentive Christian fathers—not only in Guatemala, but in any land."

18. Bishop, "Transforming Power of the Gospel," *C.A.B.* (April 1907), vol. 13, p. 4.

19. Bishop, Mar. 29, 1905, *C.A.B.* (April 1905), vol. 11, p. 14. Bishop commented that "this wonderful giving by our poor native believers has come about by a number of them having adopted the plan of giving proportionately every week or month of all their earnings. . . ."

20. A. E. Bishop, "Informes de la Iglesia de las Cinco Calles, por seis meses, Julio 1–Dec. 31, 1921," ACAM. The disbursements for the same

six-month period were as follows: for nine workers for six months, $41,-382.00; for the poor, orphans, sick, etc., $3,376.00; for repair of the chapel chairs, $468.00; for the cleaning of the chapel, $600.00; and for electricity, $573.00. These amounts are in Guatemalan money.

21. Bishop, Sept. 1, 1909, *C.A.B.* (October 1909), vol. 15, p. 6; Bishop to Mosher Manufacturing Company, Dec. 22, 1919, ACAM, Bishop to Luther Rees, Feb. 8, 1922, ACAM; Bishop, "History," p. 18; Houser, Feb. 19, 1912, *C.A.B.* (April 1912), vol. 18, p. 19; and Bishop, "Informes de la Iglesia de las Cinco Calles," ACAM.

22. Bishop, "History," p. 16. He indicated that the rainy season occurred from May to November and that the rainfall was about 150 inches during that time.

23. Bishop, Mar. 20, 1903, *C.A.B.* (April 1903), vol. 9, pp. 7–8; Bishop, June 21, 1911, *C.A.B.* (July 1911), vol. 17, pp. 6–8; and Bishop to Judge D. H. Scott, Nov. 5, 1910, ACAM.

24. Bishop, General Letter No. 69 (May 8, 1917) ACAM.

25. "Some Things About Our Work and Workers: A. E. Bishop and the Guatemala City Center," *C.A.B.* (January 1921), vol. 27, p. 6.

26. "Notes from Mr. Rees," *C.A.B.* (July 1919), vol. 25, pp. 4–5. Rees, after a visit, remarked: "At the large night service I spoke through Brother Bishop and the message was then interpreted from Spanish into Cachiquel Indian tongue by Gregorio Arroyo, one of the Indian workers."

27. "Native Churches, Sunday Schools, and Native Workers," *C.A.B.* (July 1915), vol. 21, p. 3; "Statistical Report of Our Work in Central America," *C.A.B.* (May 1921), vol. 27, p. 4; and Miss Mary A. Bishop, Sept. 7, 1921, *C.A.B.* (September 1921), vol. 27, p. 15.

28. Bishop, n.d., *C.A.B.* (March 1921), vol. 27, p. 6.

29. Bishop, July 2, 1910, *C.A.B.* (July 1910), vol. 16, p. 17; and Bishop, Dec. 3, 1908, *C.A.B.* (January 1909), vol. 15, p. 6.

30. Bishop, Nov. 25, 1913, *C.A.B.* (January 1914), vol. 20, p. 6; Bishop to Rees, Dec. 27, 1921, ACAM; and Bishop, "History," p. 17. He reminisced that "to the Guatemala Christians is due in a large measure the growth and success of the work in general."

31. Bishop, General Letter No. 78 (June 8, 1921) ACAM. He stated: "It costs as much to support a good mounted man as it does to support three or four bare-foot ones. But as the work of each is indispensable and one cannot do the work of the other we are sure that we have God's mind."

32. Bishop, Apr. 10, 1916, *C.A.B.* (July 1916), vol. 22, p. 6.

33. Bishop, Apr. 22, 1919, *C.A.B.* (May 1919), vol. 25, p. 5. On the last day of the conference seven hundred attended Sunday School.

34. Bishop, n.d., *C.A.B.* (March 1921), vol. 27, p. 5. Bishop explained that as a result of the conference in 1921, "problems were solved, offenders were forgiven, dissensions were settled, strife and envy and jealousies were forgotten...."

35. Bishop, General Letter No. 76 (Sept. 15, 1920) ACAM.

36. Bishop, June 8, 1899, *C.A.B.* vol. 5, p. 10. He indicated that when the priests interfered ". . . often the very ones that you have thought most interested are your bitterest enemies."

37. "Prayer to Our Lady of Guadalupe Against the Evangelist Sect," *C.A.B.* (October 1911), vol. 17, p. 3.

38. Miss Daisy Ifert, June 20, 1903, *C.A.B.* (July 1903), vol. 9, p. 11; and C. F. Lincoln, Apr. 18, 1911, *C.A.B.* (July 1911), vol. 17, pp. 8–9.

39. Bishop to Scott, Sept. 1, 1921, ACAM.

40. Ibid.

41. Bishop, Dec. 28, 1904, *C.A.B.* (January 1905), vol. 11, p. 12.

42. F. W. Boyle, June 15, 1896, *C.A.B.* (July 1896), vol. 2, p. 6.

43. H. C. Dillon, Feb. 6, 1897, *C.A.B.* (April 1897), vol. 3, p. 8. "The priests have taught them that the Queen supports all Protestant missionaries with the object of subjecting all nations to herself."

44. Ibid.

45. Bishop, General Letter No. 78 (June 8, 1921) ACAM.

46. Bishop, Apr. 14, 1900, *C.A.B.* (July 1900), vol. 6, p. 7; June 2, 1899, *C.A.B.* (July 1899), vol. 5, p. 10; and Aug. 5, 1899, *C.A.B.* (October 1899), vol. 5, p. 9.

47. Bishop, Oct. 20, 1899, *C.A.B.* (January 1900), vol. 6, p. 7.

48. Bishop, Jan. 13, 1900, *C.A.B.* (April 1900), vol. 6, pp. 24–25.

49. Bishop and F. G. Toms, "A Religious Mob," *C.A.B.* (July 1905), vol. 11, p. 11.

50. Ibid.

51. Ibid.

52. Ibid., p. 12.

53. Ibid.

54. Bishop, Aug. 3, 1912, *C.A.B.* (April 1912), vol. 18, p. 7; and Bishop, July 14, 1900, *C.A.B.* (October 1900), vol. 6, p. 7.

55. Bishop, Feb. 9, 1900, *C.A.B.* (April 1900), vol. 6, p. 25; and F. G. Toms, July 1, 1912, *C.A.B.* (July 1912), vol. 18, p. 9.

56. J. C. Cassel, Mar. 16, 1908, *C.A.B.* (April 1908), vol. 14, p. 13.

57. Treichler, Oct. 26, 1918, *C.A.B.* (January 1919), vol. 25, p. 6; and Bishop to Scott, Oct. 26, 1921, ACAM.

58. "Notes: A Message from Bro. Bishop," *C.A.B.* (January 1911), vol. 17, pp. 8–9. Bishop remarked in January 1911, "yesterday I commenced to re-read the Bible consecutively for something like the 18th time."

59. Bishop to Scott and Rees, June 30, 1920, ACAM.

60. Bishop to Scott, Oct. 20, 1920, ACAM. Bishop stated: "I used to think that I would have to take Mondays for a rest day, but for 3 years that has not been possible and my labors are incessant seven days to the week."

61. Bishop to Rees, Mar. 29, 1922, ACAM; and Mary A. Bishop to Scott, Sept. 7, 1921, ACAM. The missionary stated: ". . . we see the greatness of the work and the need of workers, but our strength has entirely given out and it seems absolutely necessary for us to take this rest."

8 | The Role of Aviation in Mexican-United States Relations, 1912-1929

Wesley Phillips Newton

In 1910, Francisco I. Madero initiated a rebellion against the dictatorship of Porfirio Díaz, thus setting off the bitter struggle known as the Mexican Revolution. The United States, sharing an extensive border with Mexico, naturally became entangled in its neighbor's conflict. During the years from 1912 to 1929, one significant aspect of United States–Mexican relations involved a newly developed innovation in warfare, the airplane.

In March 1912, the United States President William Howard Taft proclaimed a general embargo on shipments of arms to Mexico, on the grounds that arms and ammunition from north of the border were aggravating domestic violence south of it.[1] For the next seventeen years, this executive act was used by the United States to manipulate politics, as a diplomatic lever, and as a balm in Mexican–United States relations. Within a month after the embargo on arms and ammunition was proclaimed, the Madero government induced the United States to prevent the shipment of an airplane that, the Federals claimed, was intended to be used to drop explosives on their forces. This was the first time that aviation was involved in the various interpretations of the embargo.[2]

A United States company, acting through the Madero government, persuaded Washington, in August 1912, to allow the export of two planes and replacement parts. These were for the Federal forces operating under Victoriano Huerta against the rebels in Chihuahua. Although Taft was empowered to exempt articles from the embargo, and Washington had adopted the policy of allowing the Federals arms upon request, it is not without humor that these aviation items were allowed to go to Huerta on the State Department's ritualistic certification that they were unlikely to contribute to domestic violence.[3]

Smuggling of planes from the United States into Mexico became a regular thing. Many of the pilots and mechanics were either citizens of the United States or foreigners who had spent some time there before they served in the Mexican Revolution.

Hector Worden was the first United States mercenary to fly in the revolution. After he was employed by Madero's Federal forces, he flew patrol over rail lines and bridges and occasionally dropped bombs on rebels who threatened these communications.[4] Didier Masson, a Franco-American, took part in some of the first sensational exploits of aerial warfare in Mexico.[5] He had tried early in 1913 to smuggle a plane into Mexico from Arizona, but United States deputy marshals seized it. In a few days he crossed the border in a vehicle that carried a crated Curtiss-type pusher airplane, powered by a 75-horsepower Martin engine, which he had acquired mysteriously.[6]

The political complexion of the Revolution changed when Victoriano Huerta became president on February 19, 1913 after deposing Madero. Huerta, in turn, was soon attacked by a rebel faction known as the Constitutionalists. Under Alvaro Obregón the Constitutionalists engaged Masson and his mechanic-bombardier, a British subject named Thomas J. Dean, to fly for them. At first the flying mercenaries merely dropped propaganda leaflets, but they soon turned to deadlier work. Masson flew sorties, with either Dean or some Mexican bombardier, against two Federal warships in the Huerta-held harbor of Guaymas. Although Dean's bomb release gear was primitive and his aim poor, the Federal captains felt their ships sufficiently endangered to head for open water. Engine failure on another sortie forced Masson to land within range of hostile guns, but he and his crew escaped without injury.[7]

Later, in April 1914, Gustavo Salinas Carranza, a pioneer Mexican aviator, tried unsuccessfully to hit the Federal warships off the west coast of Mexico.[8] The following month, however, he shifted his attack to the Federal-occupied port of Mazatlán in Sinaloa. On May 3, United States vice-consul Alfred G. Brown saw an airplane "taking observations" of the city, its fort, and the harbor. When it returned on May 6, Brown and his wife climbed to the roof of the consulate to watch it. The plane released an object that Brown thought to be a piece of paper. As it "grew in velocity," Brown reported, "it was noted to be making somewhat of a noise . . . and in a moment the people, incredulous and innocent, who lived on the corner of . . . Ocampo and Carnival were thrown into a panic, for thirteen of them were wounded and three killed. . . ." [9]

The bombing of the city aroused Rear Admiral Thomas B. Howard, commander of the United States Pacific Fleet, who was in Mazatlán harbor at the time. He and the senior German naval officer on duty there arranged for a conference with Obregón's delegates. The Constitutionalists expressed regret over the civilian casualties and claimed that a faulty mechanism had released the bomb prematurely. At the insistence of the naval officers, Obregón joined the Federal commander of Mazatlán in agreeing to establish a neutral zone in that city.[10] The Constitutionalist plane, often flown by Gustavo Salinas Carranza with Dean as bombardier, returned and began to score increasingly accurate hits on the Federal strongholds in Mazatlán. The enemy was observed to have abandoned these points, but when Constitutionalist troops took the port, they discovered one large trench that contained the bodies of Federal soldiers killed in the bombing.[11]

These sorties by Masson, Dean, and Salinas Carranza were soon followed by further aerial activity in the Revolution. Almost every faction acquired a few planes. On one occasion in 1913, an unusual aerial drama took place when two of the fragile machines of the time clashed. One plane was piloted by a Constitutionalist aviator and professional adventurer, Dean Ivan Lamb, variously described as an American or a Canadian. Philip Rader, a United States national, was flying the other plane for Huerta. After their machines almost locked wings as they maneuvered, Lamb and Rader took turns firing pistols at one another, but each deliberately missed his aim. For these two men, having known each other in the United States, were willing to bomb trenches and encampments of their employers' enemies, but they did not wish to kill each other. Thus they feigned what might otherwise have been the first air-to-air combat in the western hemisphere.[12]

Another United States national who flew in revolutionary Mexico was a respected pilot, Charles F. Niles. Niles, who headed the Constitutionalist aviation section late in 1914 and in 1915, once landed in a public square in Mexico City, where he was greeted by cheering crowds. His experiences there, however, prejudiced him against the Mexicans, and on his voluntary return to the United States he claimed that their cheers had arisen from their belief that he was an advance scout for an invading United States army. Indeed, Niles believed that such an invasion was the only answer to Mexico's woes. Having lost faith in the Constitutionalist leaders, he resigned from his position as head of their air force.[13]

The ban on arms continued to affect the status of aviation in Mexico. When Woodrow Wilson became president in 1913, the embargo, although not applied to the Mexican Federal government headed by Huerta, was still in force with respect to revolutionaries. As noted, Didier Masson had to smuggle his plane into Mexico to join the Constitutionalists. Wilson, however, regarded Huerta as an evil usurper and on February 3, 1914 suspended the embargo in order to aid Venustiano Carranza, the leader of the Constitutionalists. Soon several planes, ferried by Harold Kantor and others, reached the Constitutionalists.[14]

A few weeks later, aviation played a small but significant part in an event that marked the beginning of the end for Huerta. In 1914 the Wilson government took the controversial step of ordering United States Atlantic naval forces to Mexico in order to block supplies to Huerta. Marines and bluejackets soon were fighting Mexicans in Veracruz. On April 19 the Bureau of Navigation issued an order to the officer who commanded the main concentration of United States naval aviation forces, which at that time were stationed at Pensacola, Florida. In obedience to that order, Lt. Comdr. Henry C. Mustin sent part of his small force of planes and personnel to Mexico on the scout cruiser U.S.S. *Birmingham*. Not long after he had turned his attention again to his training duties in Pensacola, he received another order directing him to load the rest of his forces aboard a makeshift aircraft carrier, the U.S.S. *Mississippi*, and to sail for Mexico.[15] The *Birmingham* had taken its first detachment of aviators to Tampico, but the *Mississippi* went to Veracruz, where it arrived on the night of April 24. On the voyage down, Mustin had his mechanics construct a landing gear for hydroplanes that made it possible to use them for shorebased operations. He also ordered his men to prepare some aerial bombs, for which they used the warheads of torpedoes as detonators.[16]

On the morning of April 25, Lt. (j.g.) P.L.N. Bellinger took off from the harbor in a hydroplane. His reconnaissance of twenty-eight minutes over the harbor and surrounding area was the first United States naval or military flight in connection with actual operations against opposing forces over disputed territory. On the initial and subsequent flights that day, the naval aviators performed valuable services for the fleet by reporting that, from their excellent vantage point, they could detect no mines in the harbor. The Mexicans who came out into the streets to stare up at the planes were as "incredulous and innocent" as their compatriots were to be at Mazatlán a few weeks later. But the United States planes kept their homemade bombs in their racks as they passed over the harbor and the bright-colored buildings of Veracruz to reconnoiter the sandhills beyond. In New York City, people unfolded the *Times* to the headline, "Our Aeroplanes Up at Vera Cruz to Locate the Foe." [17]

At Tampico, where the drama of intervention originated, the naval aviation section saw no action. But at Veracruz the flyers went up every day for several weeks, scouting the countryside for signs of enemy movement or handiwork. The men in the cockpits saw scattered bands of Mexican cavalrymen and foot soldiers, observed bridges, and took note of whether railroad tracks and ties were ripped up or in place. The information that they brought back in the first few days of flying dispelled the fear that the Mexicans might be massing for an attack on the city.[18] Secretary of the Navy Josephus Daniels was enthusiastic over the aviators' work.[19]

No bombs were dropped at Veracruz, despite at least two instances that might have justified retaliation. One provocation occured on May 2, 1914 when a United States plane made a reconnaissance flight over a vital water-pumping station held by the marines at El Tejar. Although the observers spotted no suspicious activity, after they landed they found bullet holes in the wings of their plane. Another incident took place a few weeks later, when the United States ground forces heard the rattle of Mexican small-arms fire and discovered that the shots were being directed at a low-flying plane which, fortunately, was not hit.[20]

In 1915 the political winds of the Mexican Revolution changed once again as Pancho Villa revolted against the leadership of Carranza. The airplane, frail and often underpowered for flying in the high altitudes of northern Mexico, continued to play a part in the fighting. Carranza used a small force of planes, now under the direction of another United States aviator, W. Leonard Bonney, who had replaced Charles F. Niles. With the suspension of the United States embargo in February 1914 Villa apparently had little trouble in obtaining planes to oppose those of the Constitutionalists. He was also able to recruit United States flyers, although at times he released them and let the planes lie idle.[21] There is no evidence to indicate that the airplane won any campaigns or even a battle for Pancho Villa. They did, however, make a vivid impression on the minds of Mexicans. Such an impression is reflected in *Los de Abajo*, Mariano Azuela's famous novel of the Revolution, as one of the characters speaks in awe of "Villa's Machines."

> Christ, those planes! You know when they're close to you, be damned if you know what the hell they are! They look like small boats . . . and then pretty soon they begin to rise, making a hell of a row. . . . Then they're like great big birds. . . . But there's a Joker! The god-damn things have got some American fellow inside with hand-grenades by the thousand. . . . The fight is on, see? You know how a farmer feeds corn to his chickens, huh? Well, the American throws his lead bombs at the enemy just like that. Pretty soon the[22] whole damn field is nothing but a graveyard. . . .

On October 19, 1915, two events in Washington incensed Villa: the United States government extended *de facto* recognition to the Carranza government and reimposed the arms embargo in such a way that it applied only to the area of northern Mexico where Villa's forces were concentrated.[23] The Carranza government continued to receive arms from across the border. Villa, who hoped to motivate a situation whereby only he stood to gain, ordered his agents to begin guerrilla attacks north of the border. These attacks climaxed in the raid that Villa himself led against Columbus, New Mexico, in March 1916. With the somewhat grudging and limited permission of the Carranza government, the enraged United States government sent a punitive military expedition into northern Mexico. Its cavalry and infantry forces marched across the border on March 16 to disperse Villa's forces.[24] Three days later, a small group of United States planes flew across the Mexican line and droned southward.[25]

However, United States aviation operations had begun along the border as early as 1911. In that year a few army planes were a part of the border patrol created by Taft.[26] The Huerta *coup* of February 1913 provided the impulse for stationing a small group of army planes at Texas City, Texas, and for forming the first real army tactical air unit, the First Aero Squadron.[27] Army flyers, however, merely observed the Mexican Revolution for several years. They would concentrate on the border during flare-ups in Mexican–United States tensions, such as the occupation of Veracruz, but the War Department never ordered them into Mexico.[28] In the spring and again in the summer of 1915, Signal Corps planes flying near the line drew hostile but ineffectual small-arms fire from Mexican soil. The situation became more serious in March 1916, when the First Aero Squadron was sent from Texas to Columbus, New Mexico.[29]

In many respects a stepchild of the army at that time, aviation suffered neglect. The eight JN–3 planes of the army's only tactical air unit, which flew from Columbus, were worn and their 85 and 95–horsepower motors were grossly inadequate for the rarified air and tricky wind currents of northern Mexico. One plane crash-landed on the journey south and another had to turn back. Therefore, the unit was reduced by one-fourth before it had seen action. The pilots, who operated from the shifting headquarters of the expedition's commander, Brig. Gen. John J. Pershing, flew to carry orders and dispatches to the cavalry units and diplomatic agents in the area and to investigate Mexican troop movements.[30] The squadron soon inaugurated a courier service between Pershing's base and Columbus, which contributed to the swift transmission of news and dispatches to the United States and relieved the telegraph of part of the burden.[31] The squadron's activities might have shortened the expedition's stay in Mexico if circumstances had not limited its effectiveness. The flyers, who were under the command of Capt. Benjamin D. Foulois, performed under difficult conditions. The low-powered motors often failed to lift the machines over ranges or even foothills; the flyers suffered from frostbite in the extreme cold of the upper air; and the planes were buffeted on the ground by sandstorms. A newspaper correspondent described a typical take-off of the squadron's planes: "I have seen them run along the ground like quail for a quarter of a mile before getting enough purchase on the air to lift [themselves]...."[32]

More than once the flyers had to abandon wrecked planes and take a long, thirsty hike through a barren land. Natives of the region did not welcome the flyers, nor did they understand their machines. Their suspicion was reflected by questions that they asked the Americans: "Have they glasses up there to see us? ... Can they drop big fire on us? ..." As a result of this hostility, several incidents occurred. On one occasion, after relations between the United States and Carranza became tense because of the prolonged expedition, Federal *rurales* fired at, but missed, a plane that was taking off after delivering a message to the United States vice-consul at Chihuahua City; subsequently, a Mexican crowd inflicted moderate damage on a parked plane, and on another occasion Lt. Herbert A. Dargue discovered a bullet hole in his plane after a flight.[33]

During the early part of April 1916, the squadron continued its flights, which were often lengthy and, therefore, hazardous. One by one the original planes cracked up or wore out. The flyers were exceedingly fortunate to escape the same fate. By April 19, the First Aero Squadron had lost its wings and had been ordered back to Columbus by Pershing.[34]

The flyers protested that their planes were obsolete and decrepit.[35] Pershing, too, was concerned about procuring better machines to replace those that were worn out. In the event that the conflict with Mexico should result in open hostilities, he advised the War Department that an adequate fleet of planes for use there would give the United States 'a tremendous advantage. . . ." [36] A private aviation organization in the States, called the Aero Club of America, felt that with enough planes Pershing could easily pacify the Mexican troublemakers.[37] After this organization brought pressure to bear on Washington to supply his expeditionary force with more and better machines, a few new and powerful planes eventually arrived for service in Mexico; but, unlike the original planes, they were used chiefly for training.[38] Probably one reason that Pershing's flyers never encountered opposition in the air was that a number of mercenary flyers, like Masson, had been lured away from Mexico by the war in Europe; another reason was that, after a clash between Carranza's forces and Pershing's troops, the United States tightened the embargo on shipments of arms to Mexico.[39] Consequently, Carranza found it virtually impossible to obtain any new planes or replacement parts for his tiny air force. Villa, whose aviation supplies were severely restricted by the drastic enforcement of the arms ban, was in an even worse plight because his army was scattered.[40] In view of these things, both Villa and Carranza would have found it impractical to pit airplanes against those of the First Aero Squadron.

After the withdrawal of the Pershing expedition from Mexico early in 1917, the internal conflict there waned, and Carranza seemed to be firmly entrenched as president. The experience of the United States Army aviation in Mexico had afforded only one lesson for the future: planes, like any other weapon, must be of adequate number and type to be effective.[41]

For a short period, the activities of the United States Army flyers below the border came to a temporary standstill. However, the

Mexican Constitution of 1917 presaged future difficulties between that country and the United States. In the same year, an event took place that foreshadowed the role that aviation was to play in these difficulties. A United States Army plane strayed over the border into desolate Baja California, where it made a forced landing. The Mexican authorities aided in the search for the flyers, who eventually were found alive. Afterward, the Carranza government readily consented to allow a United States party to carry out salvage operations.[42] But it was less agreeable when other such overflights occurred during the expanded flight training after the United States entered World War I. However, the friction eased as the violations tapered off. Meantime, United States intelligence and other military sources began to fear that Mexico was arming herself with many planes that were either built there or supplied by Germany.[43] These fears were unrealistic, although the Mexicans did experiment with their own engines and planes.[44]

In 1919, Mexican–United States relations deteriorated as a result of Mexico's efforts to implement its Constitution of 1917 by placing restrictions on American concessions there, especially concessions that involved oil and oil rights. In the midst of the rising tension, a rash of border violations by United States Army planes took place. In August, 1919 Lts. Paul H. Davis and Harold G. Peterson, lost their way over Chihuahua, made a forced landing and fell into the hands of bandits, who demanded that the United States ransom the officers. After part of the ransom was paid, one flyer was delivered, and the other was taken from the kidnapers. Washington exacerbated the situation by sending troops across the Mexican border to pursue the bandits and a miniature Pershing expedition took place.[45] Meanwhile, the diplomatic wrangling continued even after the American forces withdrew late in August.[46] The United States claimed the right to pursue the bandits across the border on two grounds: the ineffectual Mexican control of lawlessness and the "hot trail" doctrine. The Carranza government retorted, "No foreign force has any right to enter" Mexico.[47]

Before this controversy ended, another overflight, which had none of the comic opera aspects of the Davis-Peterson affair, had taken place. Late in August, Lts. Frederick Waterhouse and C. H. Connelly disappeared on a border patrol flight between San Diego, California, and Yuma, Arizona. Apparently without permission from the Mexican government, the governor of Baja California, Esteban

Cantú, gave the United States permission to send in a search party.[48] The search proved to be fruitless. Subsequently, from official quarters in Mexico City came accusations that the search party intended to establish a permanent United States base in Baja California, but Washington vigorously denied the accusations.[49] In October, near a bay on the peninsula, a private citizen of the United States discovered the graves of Waterhouse and Connelly. Their plane was found several miles inland. On its surface, in anticipation of death from exposure, the flyers had scratched out messages to their families. An investigation revealed that they had walked to the shore of the Gulf of California, where they were brutally murdered by a treacherous Mexican fisherman, who had apparently posed as their rescuer.[50]

A few days after the discovery of the graves two other United States Army planes flew into Baja California by mistake, and their crews were forced to land there. After several days, the flyers found their way back to civilization.[51] But the matter of the planes' return caused complicated negotiations that dragged on for over a month before the Mexican government granted the United States permission to salvage them.[52] The United States vice-consul at Ensenada, Sydney Smith, severely criticized his government's attitude and activities in this matter as well as in that of Waterhouse and Connelly. Smith charged that the search for Waterhouse and Connelly had been conducted in an arrogant and stupid manner. The flyers, he claimed, would have been found alive if the search had been better organized and if the searchers had heeded local advice. The subsequent border violation, he alleged to Secretary of State Robert Lansing, was due to the planes' lack of proper navigational equipment. After studying Smith's remarks, Secretary of War Newton D. Baker promised improved equipment, but he maintained that the War Department already had regulations to curb the border violations.[53]

The prime year for border violations by airplanes was 1919, but the violations and the hostile Mexican reactions continued in 1920 and 1921.[54] Undoubtedly, a major factor in the abnormal number of overflights and other violations was due to the increase in the number of United States army flyers that were sent to the border during the crisis between the two countries. In case of an overt conflict, the War Department planned an active role for aviation in such operations as the capture of Mexican cities.[55] In 1919 leading military figures spoke of the necessity of United States airplanes on the border. William "Billy" Mitchell, for example, stressed the danger that

Mexican aviation posed. It was rumored in diplomatic circles that the Mexicans were obtaining surplus German planes and hiring former German military flyers.[56]

In 1920, the Director of the United States Army Air Service, Maj. Gen. Charles T. Menoher, received a plan through War Department channels. Apparently formulated in the State Department's Division of Mexican Affairs, the plan received the approval of the Mexican government and the tentative approval of the chief of the division of operations in the United States War Department. It proposed that Mexico should be invited to participate in a joint border air patrol to prevent smuggling and lawlessness, for which purpose surplus United States warplanes would be sold to Mexico. One major objective of the State Department was to give United States planes "more liberty of action, a greater radius of operation, and, more especially, an immunity from the penalties incurred under our regulations when, by reason of accident or loss of direction, they are forced to make landings [in Mexico]. . . ." Menoher bluntly objected to the plan and pointed out that it was not his government's policy to sell quantities of surplus airplanes to foreign countries; besides, for the government to do so, Menoher warned, would be to play into Mexican hands.[57] Consequently, the plan was never implemented.

As relations gradually improved between the two governments during the Obregón administration following the overthrow of Carranza, the effect of military aviation on Mexican–United States relations temporarily subsided. The hiring of Ralph A. O'Neill, an ex-United States aerial ace of World War I, to head training in the Mexican air force in 1920 was indicative that relations between the two countries were improving and that aviation had played its part in the improvement.[58] In 1921, the Army Air Service changed its former attitude about selling planes below the border and advocated such sales as a way of meeting European competition there.[59] The rise of commercial aviation in the postwar era contributed greatly to this change of attitude.

For the remainder of the 1920's, aviation's role in Mexican-United States relations can be divided into three sometimes overlapping categories: commercial aviation, aviation and the embargo, aviation and the diplomacy of good will. Commercial aviation, even as in more advanced and stable countries, did not begin in earnest in Mexico until after World War I. The United States' first venture into commercial aviation in Mexico, one of the very first efforts of any nation there, came in the fall of 1920, when an aviator named George Puflea arrived in Chihuahua in a plane called the Lincoln Standard. As the representative of a Nebraska concern, he sought in a general way to promote aerial transportation. He particularly tried to interest mining companies in a more rapid form of transportation than pack animals. But he met with little success in replacing their donkeys with planes.[60]

In October 1920, the Mexican government anticipated the development of commercial aviation by issuing a decree regulating the establishment of commercial airlines. Two of its provisions, which showed the influence of the Constitution of 1917, stipulated that airline companies must be Mexican and that their personnel must agree to be in effect Mexican no matter what their true nationality might be. One of the first aviation concessions was granted to several United States citizens who used Lincoln Standard planes to fly between Mexico City, Tampico, and the oil fields.[61] The Europeans, principally the Germans, offered some competition, but they never gained a solid foothold. In 1924 the consolidation of several different companies resulted in a new American-controlled enterprise, the Compañia Mexicana de Aviación, S.A. By 1927, it had become the chief commercial airline in Mexico. The company, which was headed by an American, George Rihl, owned four two-seated Lincoln Standard planes and a Fairchild cabin plane. Four regular United States pilots performed its main activities, which consisted of irregular passenger flights and a flight to carry the payrolls from Tampico to the oil fields.[62]

While there was no inflexible United States embargo on the export of commercial aircraft to Mexico in the early 1920's, the ban on the exportation of warplanes to all Mexican factions continued from 1916 to 1922.[63] This ban was a factor in forcing the Mexican government to turn to other sources for its warplanes. It did not, however, purchase large quantities from European companies. The reason for its failure to do so lay in the fact that the Mexican appropriations for aviation were very small.[64]

But the Federal government did continue to ask Washington for warplanes, aviation accessories, and other arms when it was faced with a serious uprising by Adolfo de la Huerta in 1923–1924. The United States government accommodated President Obregón by imposing a new embargo and applying it only to the rebels.[65] During the campaign, Obregón's forces employed their planes effectively.

The federal aviators prepared the way for the seizure of a rebel stronghold by an aerial bombardment, a technique that had been refined since the bombing of Mazatlán in 1914. Airplanes, some of which were United States military types, supported other federal operations.[66] A rebel manifesto accused the Obregonistas of employing United States mercenary flyers to bomb old people and children, while United States sources accused the rebels of attempting to hire flyers in the States.[67]

After de la Huerta's movement had been crushed in 1924, the embargo remained in force. For a while even nonmilitary airplanes fell under the embargo, but they were freed for export in the summer of 1926. In spite of this relaxation, Secretary of State Frank B. Kellogg, who was no admirer of Mexican policies, tried late in 1926 to block a transaction whereby the Mexican government sought to acquire eight Douglas military planes for use against wild Yaqui Indians.[68] Half the planes had already been shipped into Mexico before an order to stop the shipments reached the frontier. Once more the United States quickly applied the embargo to all types of planes.[69]

While these events were taking place, the United States Army Air Corps was implementing a plan to win Latin American affection and admiration. The Air Corps also wished to survey Latin American air routes and aviation facilities. In December, 1926 five amphibious planes took off from Texas on a "Pan American Good Will Flight." The first stop on the courtesy visit to the nations of Latin America was Mexico. The War Department hoped that the flight would eventually lead to a United States airline, with a system of routes radiating throughout the lands to the south. The essential motive for establishing such an airline was to dominate Latin American air routes in order to forestall their control by any European aviation enterprise that would be a threat to the Panama Canal. The essence of the threat was that a potential enemy might be able to send a bomber in the guise of an airliner over the Canal. The proposed solution: the United States hoped to control the airline service in Latin America, since such a monopoly would limit the normal opportunities for European planes to fly within range of the Canal.[70]

In Mexico, the Pan American Goodwill Flight did not succeed in sowing much good will. Mexican resentment smouldered—and sometimes flared—at the intensification of United States intervention in Nicaragua, at the United States attitude toward the Mexican religious conflict, at American investments, and at the embargo. President Plutarco E. Calles was barely polite when he received the flyers. Later, after their arrival in Central America, the flight members accused the Mexicans of spreading propaganda that had aroused hostility to them at several Central American stopovers.[71]

In the midst of this rapidly deteriorating state of affairs between Mexico and the United States, President Calvin Coolidge persuaded his old friend, Dwight W. Morrow, a House of Morgan banker, to head our embassy in Mexico City. The Mexicans anticipated the arrival of the new ambassador by adopting the slogan "After Morrow the Marines." Although Morrow failed to solve many basic diplomatic problems, he did justify Coolidge's hope that he might be able to bring about an improvement in Mexican feeling toward the United States. In the placating process, Morrow successfully combined aviation with other forms of diplomacy.

He was in Washington in the summer of 1927, and there he met Charles A. Lindbergh, who had recently returned from his transatlantic flight. After Morrow's appointment to Mexico, he got the flyer's assent to a proposed flight to that country, only to have the State Department oppose the idea, possibly because of the goodwill flight's cold reception the year before. Early in December 1927, the State Department changed its mind. Not only were past objections to the flight withdrawn, Undersecretary of State Robert E. Olds informed Morrow, but it also might even have "distinct advantages . . . at this juncture. . . ." Olds did not specify what these advantages were, but he suggested that the flight might be extended to Central America,[72] an area where a slight penetration by European aviation interests had already caused United States officials to fear for the Panama Canal. Moreover, the State Department's change of mind was communicated to Morrow less than a week after Coolidge and his cabinet approved a far-reaching recommendation by a conference of executive department representatives. The government was to encourage a commercial airline to extend into Latin America. Special favor was to be given this airline in order that it dominate Latin American air routes for economic reasons and military advantage; that is, the protection of the Canal.[73]

There is evidence that the Lindbergh flight to Mexico (and subsequently to Central America, Panama, Colombia, Venezuela, Puerto Rico, Haiti, the Dominican Republic, and Cuba) had a second unpublicized official mission in addition to its goodwill mission in behalf of Morrow's diplomacy. It would have been logical strategy to utilize Lindbergh's great popularity and status as a flyer to smooth the way psychologically for the extension of an airline into Latin America. Lindbergh, writing in *The National Geographic* a short time after his return from Latin America, stated that he had been "particularly interested in the feasibility of Pan American airlines; consequently, when I received an invitation from the President of Mexico . . . it required less than a week" to prepare for the flight. Lindbergh, who covered his own flight for the *New York Times*, strongly advocated an airline to link the United States with Mexico and other countries of Latin America. He repeated this point in dispatches throughout the journey, and emphasized its importance to Latin American officials.[74] The Yankee hero visited regions that guarded the approaches to the Panama Canal or that were serviced by European-controlled airlines. It was into those areas that Pan American Airways, the chosen instrument of United States policy, would first extend its service.[75]

In December 1927, Lindbergh flew to Mexico. After losing his way, and in some respects encountering more difficulties than he did on his transatlantic flight, he arrived in Mexico City on December 14. The people showed a special affection for the celebrity, and motorcycle policemen had to form a circular barrier to protect him and his silver Ryan monoplane, *The Spirit of St. Louis*, from a huge crowd. In marked contrast to the reception of the earlier Pan American Goodwill flyers, Calles, who had already been appeased by the astute Morrow, was cordial in his greeting of Lindbergh, whose flight the Mexican executive declared to be a "priceless embassy of good will." Although Lindbergh was Nordic, the Latins found him *simpático*. He visited famous places, gave Calles and Obregón rides in his plane, and appeared in the Chamber of Deputies, where he received praise as a messenger of goodwill. Even when Obregón seized upon one of Lindbergh's public appearances to attack the "yellow press" in the United States, he lauded the flyer.[76]

One immediate result of Lindbergh's flight to Mexico was the suggestion of Representative Edith Nourse Rogers of Massachusetts that in recognition of the change in the attitude of the Calles government, which had been demonstrated by the flyer's enthusiastic reception in Mexico, the United States should lift the embargo on plane shipments to that country. This move, she felt, would not only cement the friendly relations that now existed with Mexico, but it would also help toward establishing a more extensive air service between Mexico and the United States.[77] When the State Department asked Morrow's advice on her proposal, he agreed that the embargo on airplanes should be lifted. Washington, however, was not yet ready to go that far. But in December, 1927 the ban on the shipment of civil aircraft to Mexico was informally lifted, and in March, 1928 the embargo on such planes was officially removed.[78]

Undoubtedly, Lindbergh's Mexican visit not only helped Morrow to establish better rapport with the Calles government, but it also served to effect a generally progressive improvement in relations. A specific sign of such improvement was a return goodwill flight to the United States, which was made in the summer of 1928 by a Mexican army captain, Emilio Carranza. He received a fitting welcome in Washington. In an appropriate and symbolic gesture, he flew his plane side by side with Lindbergh's. However, Carranza's goodwill flight ended in tragedy for him: his plane crashed on the way back to Mexico, and he was killed.[79] But his death brought so many sincere expressions of sorrow from people in the United States that the Mexicans seemed to realize that, despite its tragic end, his flight had achieved its goal, which was the promotion of goodwill.[80]

Two benefits of a commercial nature ensued from these various goodwill efforts. On October 1, 1928, a private United States mail contractor extended air mail service to the border. At Laredo, Texas, the service was linked with the Mexican government's official airmail line, extending from Mexico City to Nuevo Laredo. The second benefit came when, with relative ease, Pan American Airways acquired a subsidiary, the veteran line Compañia Mexicana de Aviación, S.A., in order to get around the Mexican law prohibiting foreign lines from carrying mail within Mexico. The latter's president, George Rihl, who had influence with Mexican politicians, became a vice-president of Pan American. Lindbergh, who had become a technical adviser to Pan American, flew the inaugural run of the new service between Brownsville, Texas, and Mexico City in March 1929.[81] Calles had earlier sent Coolidge a telegram in which he hailed an airline connection as a "new spirit looking toward better relations" between the two countries.[82]

Early in 1929, a revolt broke out against Calles' successor, Emilio Portes Gil. During the hostilities rebel bombs fell on United States soil several times. They were probably dropped there unintentionally, and fortunately they caused no serious casualties or great outcries.[83] The United States, however, once more used the embargo to favor Mexico's Federal government. Portes Gil's forces obtained bombs and other aviation equipment from the United States government, as well as planes from private American firms. Although the rebels could not legally buy even commercial aircraft in the United States,[84] they succeeded in smuggling warplanes across the border and in enlisting private United States citizens to fly them. Portes Gil dispelled Washington's apprehensions about having United States nationals involved in the conflict with the assurance that if such mercenary flyers were captured by Federal forces they would be treated with consideration.[85] Federal aviators made extensive use of aircraft acquired from the United States, and their warplanes contributed to the defeat of the rebels by May 1929.[86]

By July 1929, the violent phase of the Mexican Revolution seemed to have come to an end. In that month President Herbert Hoover signed a proclamation terminating the United States embargo, thus ending the controversies over the shipment of planes across the border and removing a prime source of Mexico's resentment towards the United States.[87] Although the airplane's major role had been as an instrument of violence in a turbulent period of United States-Mexican relations, this role began to change as the violence of the revolution subsided. Increasing air traffic would facilitate communications, thus promoting a more cordial relationship.

Notes

1. Presidential Proclamation No. 1158, Mar. 14, 1912, in *Papers Relating to the Foreign Relations of the United States, 1912* (Washington: Government Printing Office, 1919), pp. 745–746. Taft's proclamation was based on a joint resolution of Congress issued the same date, which authorized the president to declare such an embargo.

2. Telegram of Henry L. Stimson to Philander C. Knox, Mar. 31, 1912, file 812.113/276; Franklin MacVeagh to Knox, Apr. 1, 1912, file 812.113/283; A. E. Wuppermann to Knox, July 17, 1912, file 812.113/768, Record Group 59, Diplomatic Branch, National Archives, Washington, D.C. (Record Groups of the National Archives hereinafter referred to as R/G. Diplomatic Branch hereinafter referred to as DB–NA.)

3. Telegram of Moisant International Aviators to W. H. Taft, Aug. 15, 1912, file 812.113/836; and Alvey A. Adee to Taft, Aug. 15, 1912, and telegram of Knox to American Consul, Nuevo Laredo, Mexico, Aug. 16, 1912, both in file 812.113/832, R/G 59, DB–NA.

4. Haldeen Brady, *Cock of the Walk* (Albuquerque: University of New Mexico Press, 1955), p. 98; Elsbeth E. Freudenthal, "How Aviation 'Firsts' Took Place in Mexico," *The Americas* (July 1947), vol. 4, p. 104;

and C. G. Grey, ed., *Jane's All the World's Aircraft, 1917* (London: Sampson Low, Marston & Company, 1917), p. 194b. (hereinafter referred to as *Jane's*).

5. *Jane's* states that Masson was born in France, but the United States was his adopted country. (*Jane's*, 1917, p. 194b.)

6. Note of J.B. Moore to A. Algara R. de Terreros, May 20, 1913, file 812.00/7514, R/G 59, DB–NA; *New York Times*, May 9 and 20, 1913; and Southern Department Report No. 10 of Brig. Gen. Tasker H. Bliss to War Department, May 31, 1913, adjutant general file, R/G 94, Army and Navy Section, War Record Branch, National Archives (hereinafter this section is referred to as ANS-WRB-NA).

7. *New York Times*, May 31, 1913; dispatch of Alfred Gordon Brown to William Jennings Bryan, May 6, 1914, file 812.00/12034, R/G 59, DB-NA; "Mexico," *The Aeroplane*, (July 17, 1913), vol. 5, p. 70; and *New York Times*, June 22 and Aug. 11, 1913.

8. John W. F. Dulles, *Yesterday in Mexico* (Austin: University of Texas Press, 1961), p. 7; and Doroteo Negrete, *Historia de la aeronáutica en México* [also titled *Cronología Aeronáutica de México*] (México, D.F., n.d.), pp. 44–45.

9. Brown to Bryan, May 6, 1914, file 812.00/12034, R/G 59, DB-NA.

10. Report with appendices of Rear Admiral T.B. Howard to secretary of navy (Operations), July 7, 1914, file 812.00/13075, R/G 59, DB-NA.

11. "Bomb Dropping with Carranza," [British] *Aeronautics*, New Series. (Dec. 1, 1915), vol. 9, pp. 364–365; and "Mexico," *The Aeroplane*, p. 70.

12. Dean Ivan Lamb, *The Incurable Filibuster* (New York: Farrar & Rinehart, Inc., 1934), pp. 90–95.

13. Report of Brig. Gen. R.K. Evans to Southern Department, United States Army, Nov. 10, 1914, file 812.24/31, R/G 59, DB-NA; *New York Times*, Mar. 29, 1915; Negrete, *Historia*, pp. 45–47; "Niles Quits Mexico," *Aerial Age Weekly* (Apr. 5, 1915), vol. 1, p. 64; and "Bomb Dropping with Carranza," *Aeronautics*, p. 364.

14. Presidential Proclamation, Feb. 3, 1914, file 812.113/31105a, R/G 59, DB-NA; and *New York Times*, Apr. 3, 1914.

15. Report of H.C. Mustin to commander in chief, U.S. Atlantic Fleet, May 19, 1914, ANS-WRB-NA (hereinafter this report is referred to as Mustin Report).

16. Log of the U.S.S. *Mississippi*, entry of Apr. 24, 1914, p. 298, ANS-WRB-NA; and Mustin Report.

17. Mustin Report; and *New York Times*, Apr. 26, 1914.

18. Mustin Report; and *New York Times*, Apr. 26, 27, 28, and 30, 1914.

19. Report No. 93, Navy Department, n.d., and Mustin to Mark L. Bristol, May 30, 1914, Mark L. Bristol Papers, Manuscript Division, Library of Congress.

20. "Aviators at Work at Vera Cruz," *Army and Navy Journal* (May 9, 1914), vol. 51, p. 1150; and extract from telegram of Brig. Gen. Fred-

erick Funston to Agwar, May 24, 1914, file 812.00/12089, R/G 59, DB-NA.

21. "Scouting Trip over the City of Mexico," *Aerial Age Weekly* (Dec. 13, 1915), vol. 2, p. 309; "Bonney Back Seeking New Aeroplanes for Mexico," *Aerial Age Weekly* (June 21, 1915), vol. 1, 319; and Negrete, *Historia*, pp. 46–53; *Jane's, 1917*, p. 194b; report of Gaston Schmaltz to Bryan, May 6, 1915, file 812.00/15014; and Schmaltz to Bryan, May 3, 1915, file 812.00/14997, R/G 59, DB-NA. Although the first true airplane flight in Mexico had taken place in 1910, native civil aviation development took a back seat to military development. At the prompting of pioneer Mexican aviator Alberto Salinas Carranza, the Mexican Federal government in 1915 established a military flying school and factory near Mexico City. When the war in Europe and embargo in the United States made it difficult to obtain airplanes, the Mexicans began to produce other foreign models of aircraft on license and, in a few years turned out a Mexican military type in small numbers. See José Villela Jr., "Heroes y Hazañas en la Historia de la Aviación Mexicana," *Aviación*, no. 14 (November, 1959); "Alberto Braniff y el Cincuentenario de la Aviación en México," *Aviación*, nos. 15–16 (December 1959–January 1960); *Jane's, 1928*, pp. 29b and 175c.

22. Mariano Azuela, *The Under Dogs* (New York: Brentano's, 1929), pp. 109–110.

23. Note of Robert Lansing to E. Arredondo, Oct. 19, 1915, file 812.00/16532b; and memorandum of Stephen Latchford to Lansing, Aug. 7, 1916, file 812.113/4679, R/G 159, DB-NA.

24. Howard F. Cline, *The United States and Mexico* (Cambridge: Harvard University Press, 1953), pp. 174–178; and Clarence C. Clendenen, *The United States and Pancho Villa: A Study in Unconventional Diplomacy* (Ithaca: Cornell University Press, 1961), p. 317. Clendenen maintains that the Pershing punitive expedition mission was, first and foremost, to disperse Villa's forces and that it was successful.

25. Report of Capt. Benjamin B. Foulois on "Operations of the First Aero Squadron, Signal Corps with the Punitive Expedition, U.S.A., for the period March 15 to August 15, 1916," file 168.65011–7A, United States Air Force Historical Division Archives, Maxwell Air Force Base, Alabama. (Archives hereinafter referred to as USAFHDA, and this report referred to as Foulois Report.)

26. Freudenthal, "How Aviation 'Firsts' took Place," pp. 101–102.

27. Juliette A. Hennessey, "The United States Army Air Arm, April 1861 to April 1917," USAF Historical Division Studies: No. 98 (Maxwell AFB: Research Studies Institute, 1958), p. 74; and Sq-Bombl [-] Hi-Mar. 1913–Dec. 1916, unpublished manuscript, USAFHDA.

28. Hennessey, "United States Army Air Arm," pp. 78–79 and 105–106.

29. "Carranza Soldiers Fire on U.S. Aviators," *Aerial Age Weekly* (May 3, 1915), vol. 1, p. 152; telegram of Funston to adjutant general, Sept. 2, 1915, adjutant general file, R/G 94, ANS-WRB-NA; and Foulois Report.

30. Foulois Report.

31. *New York Times*, Mar. 25 and 28 and Apr. 1, 1916.

32. Foulois Report; Henry A. Woodhouse, "No Aeroplanes for Mexican Campaign," *Flying* (April 1916), vol. 5, pp. 101–102; "Government Aeros Not Suitable for Mexico," *Aerial Age Weekly* (April 3, 1916), vol. 3, p. 95; "More Aeros and Larger Engines for the Mexican Campaign," *Aerial Age Weekly* (April 10, 1916), vol. 3, p. 116; and Gregory Mason, "The Doughboy and the Truck, Some Lessons of our Mexican Expedition," *Outlook* (May 31, 1916), vol. 113, p. 282.

33. *New York Times*, Apr. 1, 1916; Foulois Report; and Woodhouse, "No Aeroplanes for Mexican Campaign, *Flying* (May 1916), vol. 2, p. 151.

34. Foulois Report; and Funston to adjutant general, Apr. 19, 1916, adjutant general file, R/G 94, ANS-WRB-NA.

35. Telegram of Funston to adjutant general, Apr. 27, 1916; and second endorsement of George P. Scriven, May 18, 1916, to telegram of Funston to adjutant general, May 16, 1916, adjutant general's file, R/G 94, ANS-WRB-NA.

36. Funston to adjutant general, Apr. 18, 1916, adjutant general's file, R/G 94, ANS-WRB-NA.

37. Alan R. Hawley to Newton D. Baker, Mar. 14, 1916, adjutant general's file, R/G 94, ANS-WRB-NA; and Alan R. Hawley, "The Need of Building our Aeronautical Industry to Create Sources of Supply of Aircraft for National Defense," *Aerial Age Weekly* (Feb. 19, 1917), vol. 4, p. 649.

38. Foulois Report; Frederick Palmer, *Newton D. Baker: America at War* (New York: Dodd, Mead, & Co., 1931), vol. 1, p. 283.

39. Telegram of adjutant general to Funston, May 1, 1916, file 812.113/4115; memorandum of Latchford to Lansing, Aug. 7, 1916, file 812.113/4679, R/G 59, DB–NA; and Cline, *United States and Mexico*, p. 181.

40. Guy Kilpatric, "Aviation in Mexico," *The Aeroplane* (Jan. 10, 1917), vol. 12, p. 188.

41. "Observation Aviation," mimeographed textbook, Air Corps Tactical School, Maxwell Field, Alabama, July, 1937, p. 7, file 248.10112, USAFHDA. This document states that the flesh was willing and able, but the struts, wings, engines, etc., were too weak, so no valuable lessons were learned.

42. Telegram of William A. Glassford to chief signal officer, Jan. 20, 1917 and Frederick Simpich to Robert Lansing, Jan. 17, 1917, adjutant general file, R/G 94, ANS-WRB-NA; and Lansing to Baker, Mar. 7, 1917, file 811.2313/2, R/G 59, DB-NA.

43. Note of Samuel A. Gibson to collector of customs, Los Angeles, California, July 30, 1917, file 812.796; and Tom F. Furlong to Lansing, June 13, 1918, file 812.24/60, R/G 59, DB-NA.

44. *Jane's, 1928*, p. 175c.

45. *New York Times*, Aug. 18, 19, 20, and 21, 1919; Clendenen, *The United States and Pancho Villa*, pp. 312–313; and Stacy C. Hinkle, *Wings and Saddles: The Air and Cavalry Punitive Expedition of 1919*, South-

western Studies, vol. 5, no. 3 (El Paso: Texas Western Press, 1967), pp. 8–38.

46. *New York Times,* Aug. 26, 1919.

47. Note of Lansing to Y. Bonillas, Aug. 26, 1919, file 812.0144/151; and Bonillas to William Phillips, Sept. 23, 1919, file 812.0144/184, R/G 59, DB-NA.

48. *New York Times,* Oct. 3, 1919; and note of Baker to Lansing, Oct. 6, 1919, file 812.0144/188, R/G 59, DB-NA.

49. *New York Times,* Oct. 5, 1919; and Lansing to Summerlin, Oct. 16, 1919, file 812.0144/182, R/G 59, DB-NA.

50. *New York Times,* Oct. 27, 1919; Maj. Henry H. Arnold, "The History of Rockwell Field," unpublished manuscript, 1923, file 168.65041, USAFHDA, pp. 87–91; and Arnold, *Global Mission* (New York: Harper & Brothers, 1949), p. 91.

51. Dispatch of Sydney Smith to Lansing, Oct. 20, 1919, file 812.0144/197; and Smith to Lansing, Oct. 21, 1919, file 812.0144/208, R/G 59, DB-NA.

52. Notes of Baker to Lansing, Oct. 24, 1919 and Adee to Baker, Nov. 1, 1919, both in file 812.0144/201; telegram of Walter F. Boyle to Lansing, Oct. 30, 1919, file 812.0144/203; and Summerlin to Lansing, Nov. 23, 1919, file 812.0144/215, R/G 59, DB-NA.

53. Dispatch of Smith to Lansing, Oct. 21, 1919 and Lansing to Baker, Nov. 8, 1919 both in file 812.0144/208; and Baker to Lansing, Nov. 14, 1919, file 812.0144/213, R/G 59, DB-NA.

54. Note of Adee to S. Diego-Fernández, May 14, 1920, file 812.0144/259; Baker to Bainbridge Colby, Feb. 23, 1921, file 812.0144/278; and note of Henry P. Fletcher with enclosure to John W. Weeks, Mar. 19, 1921, file 812.0144/280, R/G 59, DB-NA.

55. Memorandum of Col. Peter Murray to Director of Air Service, Sept. 13, 1919; and Maj. Gen. Charles T. Menoher to chief, War Plans Division, General Staff, Sept. 20, 1919, Border Activities, file 370.02, R/G 18, ANS-WRB-NA.

56. Memorandum of Brig. Gen. William Mitchell to Chief, Supply Group, Air Service, July 2, 1919, Border Activities, file 370.02, R/G 18, ANS-WRB-NA; and telegram of Franklin M. Gunther to Lansing, Dec. 10, 1919, file 812.24/101, R/G 59, DB-NA.

57. Memorandum of Charles M. Johnston to Joseph R. Baker, Apr. 21, 1920, and of Colby to Joseph R. Baker, Apr. 22, 1920, both in file 812.00/23538, R/G 59, DB-NA; and endorsement of Menoher [May 4 or May 24] to letter of Colby to Baker [April 22 or May 22], Border Activities, file 370.02, R/G 18, ANS-WRB-NA. The writer has found two identical copies of Menoher's endorsement, but they have different dates. He has failed to locate the original. It is likely that the dates May 4 and April 22 are correct.

58. Aeronautical Chamber of Commerce, comp., *Aircraft Year Book, 1922* (New York, 1922), p. 90 (hereinafter referred to as *Year Book*); and *New York Times,* Aug. 21, 1920.

59. Memorandum of Office of Chief of Air Service to adjutant general,

Feb. 15, 1921, Foreign Aviation Reports, Italy to South America [Mexico], file 360.02, R/G 18, ANS-WRB-NA (hereinafter referred to as Reports, Italy to South America).

60. Dispatch of James B. Stewart to Colby, Oct. 29, 1920, file 812.796/6, R/G 59, DB-NA.

61. Dispatch of Cornelius Ferris, Jr., to Colby, Nov. 3, 1920, file 812.-796/7; *Diario Oficial*, Oct. 18, 1920; and report of Claude I. Dawson to Hughes, Aug. 10, 1921, file 812.796/11, R/G 59, DB-NA.

62. Dispatch of Stewart to Hughes, Dec. 9, 1924, file 812.796/15; John Q. Wood to Frank B. Kellogg, Mar. 7, 1927, file 812.796/20; Arthur C. Frost to Kellogg, Mar. 12, 1927, file 812.796/21; dispatch of Wood to Kellogg, Mar. 22, 1927, file 812.796/22; report of Fayette J. Flexer to Kellogg, May 19, 1927, file 812.796/26; Dudley G. Dwyre to State Department, May 10, 1929, file 812.796/50, R/G 59, DB-NA; and *Year Book, 1929*, p. 220.

63. Dispatch of Fletcher to Lansing, June 5, 1917, file 711.12/50; Presidential Proclamation, July 9, 1917, file 600.119/223a; Frank L. Polk to Woodrow Wilson, July 9, 1919, and Presidential Proclamation No. 1530, July 12, 1919, file 612.11/2623a; regulations of the Department of State, May 1, 1920, file 612.119/2854; telegram of Fletcher to Summerlin, Mar. 3, 1922, file 812.113/9306a; and Hughes to Summerlin, Mar. 7, 1922, file 812.113/9307, R/G 59, DB-NA.

64. *Year Book, 1923*, pp. 183–184; *Year Book, 1926*, pp. 175–176; and *Year Book, 1928*, pp. 226–227.

65. Notes of Manuel C. Téllez to Hughes, Jan. 4 and Feb. 5, 1924, file 812.24/202 and 250 respectively; and Presidential Proclamation No. 1683, Jan. 7, 1924, file 812.113/9398, R/G 59, DB-NA.

66. Memorandum of Jacob E. Fickel to chief, Property Requisition Section, Feb. 18, 1924, file 452.1–3295—Sales of Planes Abroad, February 1930–July 1919 to 452.1–33—Loan of Airplanes, January 1938–August 1919, R/G 18, ANS-WRB-NA. [Materials in the Army-Navy Section of the National Archives are sometimes catalogued with dates in reverse order as given above.]; and *Year Book, 1924*, p. 211.

67. Dulles, *Yesterday in Mexico*, pp. 226, 250, 254, 259; and letter with enclosures of W. J. Burns to M.E. Hanna, Jan. 7, 1924, file 812.113/9401, R/G 59, DB-NA.

68. *New York Times*, Dec. 28, 1927; and Kellogg to Calvin Coolidge, Dec. 16, 1926 and note of Kellogg to Téllez, Dec. 16, 1926, file 812.24/477, R/G 59, DB-NA.

69. Dispatch of James R. Sheffield to Kellogg, Dec. 29, 1926 and memorandum of R. C. Tanis, Jan. 8, 1927, file 812.248/10, R/G 59, DB-NA.

70. F. Trubee Davison to Kellogg, Aug. 26, 1926, Reports, Italy to South America; Official Report of the Pan American Flight, n.d., file C71.6—Pan American Flight, Dec. 21, 1926–May 2, 1927, Central Decimal Files (1917–1938), ANS-WRB-NA, p. 1; and Wesley Phillips Newton, "International Aviation Rivalry in Latin America, 1919–1927," *Journal of Inter-American Studies* (July 1965), vol. 7, pp. 352–355.

71. Official Report of the Pan American Flight, pp. 291–297; and Ira C.

Eaker to Mason M. Patrick, Jan. 22, 1927, Selected Documents Regarding Pan American Flight, file 373, R/G 18, ANS-WRB-NA. Commander of the Pan American Flight was Maj. Herbert E. Dargue, a veteran of service with the First Aero Squadron in Mexico.

72. Harold Nicolson, *Dwight Morrow* (New York: Harcourt Brace and Company, 1935), p. 311; and telegram of Robert E. Olds to Dwight W. Morrow, Dec. 3, 1927, file 811.79612L64/1, R/G 59, DB-NA.

73. Minutes of the First Meeting of the Interdepartmental Aviation Committee, Nov. 23, 1927, and memorandum of F.B.K. [Frank B. Kellogg] to Francis White, Nov. 29, 1927, file 813.796/127; and memorandum of Joseph W. Stinson to Stimson, Mar. 7, 1931, file 810.796/35½, R/G 59, DB-NA.

74. Col. Charles A. Lindbergh, "To Bogota and Back by Air," *The National Geographic Magazine* (May 1928), vol. 53, p. 529; *New York Times*, Dec. 16, 17, 21, and 23, 1927, and Jan. 9, 1928; and dispatch of John F. Martin to Kellogg, Jan. 14, 1928, file 811.79612L64/153, R/G 59, DB-NA.

75. At the time, a Colombian-based but German-controlled airline called SCADTA was bringing pressure on the United States government to allow it use of the Canal Zone as a stopover in a projected extension of its service northward to Central America, Cuba, and the United States. See Newton, "International Aviation Rivalry in Latin America, 1919–27," pp. 353–356.

76. *New York Times*, Dec. 15, 16, 17, 18, 21, 23, and 25, 1927; and *Discursos Pronunciados En La Sesión Solemne Efectuada Por La Cámara De Diputados En Honor Del Aviador Norte-Americano Coronel Charles A. Lindbergh*, México, D.F., 1928.

77. *New York Times*, Dec. 26, 1927; and Remarks of Edith Nourse Rogers, *Congressional Record*, 70th Cong., 2d Sess., vol. 70, pt. 1, 965.

78. Telegram of Kellogg to Morrow, Dec. 21, 1927, file 812.24/655a; Morrow to Kellogg, Dec. 24, 1927, file 812.24/656; and Kellogg to Morrow, Mar. 23, 1928, file 812.113/10378a, R/G 59, DB-NA.

79. "Successful Flight of Mexico's Lone Eagle," *Bulletin of the Pan American Union* (July 1928), vol. 62, p. 703; and *New York Times*, June 13, 14, and 19, July 1, 14, 15, 16, 17, 18, 19, 22, 23, 27, and 29, and Aug. 7 and 19, 1928.

80. Gov. A. Harry Moore to Kellogg, Dec. 12, 1928, file 811.79612Carranza/150; report of Maj. Harold Thompson to assistant chief of staff, G–2, War Department, July 24, 1928, file 811.79612Carranza/139, R/G 59, DB-NA.

81. W. Irving Glover to White, Mar. 23, 1928, file 811.71212/60, R/G 59, DB-NA; *New York Times*, Oct. 2 and 3, 1928; Matthew Josephson, *Empire of the Air* (New York: Harcourt Brace and Company, 1944), pp. 49–50; report of Dwyre to State Department, May 10, 1929, file 812.796/50; Robert Harnden to State Department, July 2, 1929, file 812.796/53, R/G 59, DB-NA; and *El Universal*, July 10, 1929.

82. Telegram of Plutarco E. Calles to Coolidge, Oct. 1, 1928, file 811.-71212/66, R/G 59, DB-NA.

83. Telegram of John E. Jones to Stimson, Apr. 2, 1929, file 812.00-Sonora/490; and Jones to Stimson, Apr. 4, 1929, file 812.00Sonora/507, R/G 59, DB-NA.

84. Telegram of Morrow to Kellogg, Mar. 4, 1929, file 812.00Sonora/48; Kellogg to Morrow, Feb. 16, 1929, file 812.00Sonora/15; Morrow to Kellogg, Feb. 18, 1929, file 812.00Sonora/18; memorandum of Brig. Gen. E. E. Booth to assistant chief of staff, G–2, Jan. 11, 1929, file 812.24/927; and telegram of Kellogg to Morrow, Mar. 8, 1929, file 812.113/10455b, R/G 59, DB-NA.

85. Telegram of John W. Dye to Stimson, Apr. 1, 1929, file 812.113/10500; and Morrow to Stimson, Apr. 5, 1929, file 812.00Sonora/514, R/G 59, DB-NA.

86. Dispatch of Morrow to Stimson, May 21, 1929, file 812.00Sonora/968, R/G 59, DB-NA.

87. Telegram of Stimson to Morrow, July 2, 1929, file 812.113/10567a; and note with enclosure of J. P. Cotton to all United States consular officers in Mexico, Aug. 8, 1929, file 812.113/10580a, R/G 59, DB-NA. The sale of certain types of United States military planes to Mexico remained subject to the general restrictions on the sale of such planes abroad.

9 | The Caribbean–Vital Link in Western Hemisphere Air Defense During World War II

Herman Hupperich

The Caribbean has been a vital link in the defense of the Americas for more than one hundred years. This fact was demonstrated on several occasions in the nineteenth and twentieth centuries, but never more dramatically than during World War II. The European and Asian conflicts that raged in the 1930s placed heavy burdens on the shoulders of Western diplomats and military strategists. It became clear that the safety of the United States rested on vital decisions that had to be made quickly, and many of the more important of them involved the Caribbean area.

Early in 1939, the United States Army War College made a secret study of the forces that would be required to protect the Caribbean area from Nazi encroachment. Within ten weeks after its initial meeting, the war college advised Congress to create immediately a specially equipped Hemisphere Defense Force of 112,000 men.[1] President Franklin D. Roosevelt insisted that the steps toward military preparation be linked with the overall aims of the Good Neighbor Policy. As one means of accomplishing this, he sent Gen. George C. Marshall, United States Army Chief of Staff, on a goodwill tour of the Caribbean in the spring of 1939.

Important groundwork for the United States' acquisition and use of strategic bases in the Caribbean area was laid in 1903 by a treaty with the newly established nation of Panama.[2] Though the United States obtained minor tracts of land in Panama during and immediately after World War I, the workability of the acquisition procedure provided for in the 1903 treaty received its most severe test in the 1930s when the United States moved to acquire air bases in the Republic.

As early as January 1939, the Panama Canal Department recognized the urgent need for bases in other parts of the Caribbean region. These bases would permit advance warning of an enemy attack and would enable the Army Air Corps to engage hostile aircraft before they could strike the Canal. Nature had favored the Caribbean area by providing a chain of islands extending from Cuba southeast to the northern coast of Venezuela. These islands offered natural sites for air bases to guard the Caribbean approaches to the Panama Canal.

In September 1940, Great Britain, in exchange for fifty naval destroyers, agreed to grant air-base rights to the United States in six of Britain's Caribbean possessions stretching from the Bahamas through the Antilles to the northern coast of South America: the Bahamas, Saint Lucia, Trinidad, British Guiana, Jamaica, and Antigua.[3] In order to facilitate negotiations with the local governments, the United States and Great Britain signed an agreement in March 1941 for the use of the bases in British territories.[4]

During the spring of 1941, Maj. Gen. Frank M. Andrews, commander of the Panama Canal Department's air force, was in the final stages of molding the various air units of the Caribbean area into a well-integrated organization. The emergence of the Caribbean air force in May 1941 was a significant event involving United States defense operations, now extended to include military bases in foreign countries. Upon assuming command in September of the newly created Caribbean Defense Command, Andrews became the principal representative of the Caribbean theater in the negotiations with foreign governments for Latin American air bases.[5]

In the acquisition of installations in Central and South America and the Antilles, the commanding general of the Caribbean Defense Command relied on informal agreements with the various heads of government. In each case the arrangement depended on the circumstances existing within the country concerned. A formal pact was reached with Cuba, but in other cases the negotiations resulted in informal written agreements or simply in verbal understandings.[6]

These were necessary wartime expedients and the terms of the agreements were projected to the termination of hostilities. In the cases of Costa Rica and Nicaragua, leases were not executed with private companies until the appropriate government officials had been notified and proper authorization received. The Army Air Corps sent representatives to French Guiana and the Dutch possessions of Aruba and Curaçao upon the invitation of the home governments of France and the Netherlands. Informal arrangements were then made with the local colonial officials for the establishment of the air bases.[7]

In the spring of 1940, War Department personnel conducted an investigation to determine the possibility of developing and improving essential airports in the Caribbean with the assistance of commercial companies, such as Pan American Airways. As early as 1928, Pan American began seeking airport concessions in Latin America as a result of the initiation of flights to Cuba a year earlier. Whereas Cuba had been the only Latin American nation served by Pan American in 1928, the company during 1929 had established airports across the West Indies, through Central America, and on the South American mainland. Charles A. Lindbergh, technical advisor for Pan American, surveyed and extended the West Indies route through the Leeward Islands, the Windward Islands, and from Trinidad to the British and Dutch Guianas. By 1939, Pan American Clipper service had sketched out a route from the United States to Africa and was operating from more than two hundred bases throughout Latin America.

Officials of the United States Army suggested that Pan American Airways be entrusted with the improvement and development of bases. It was reasoned that this procedure would be more economical and less likely to create unfavorable publicity, because the improvements could be attributed to the introduction of larger types of commercial land-based aircraft. After a series of meetings between Pan American officials and United States government personnel, the secretary of war signed a contract with Pan American in November 1940 for what was called the Airport Development Program. Before the project was completed, the United States spent eighty-nine million dollars on a total of forty-eight land, sea, and air bases in Latin American countries.[8]

Because of security reasons and political complications, the State Department believed it impractical to obtain the desired Latin American facilities directly from the governments involved. It was agreed by all parties concerned that Pan American would conduct the program, ostensibly as a commercial endeavor. Since the United States at that time was not at war, discretion and secrecy were of prime consideration. Only a few key Pan American officials and United States representatives in Latin America were aware of the details of the Airport Development Program.

It was understandably difficult for Pan American to accept the responsibilities entailed by the contract. Juan Trippe, president of Pan American, feared that his company might jeopardize its excellent reputation of several years standing in the Americas by undertaking such a venture. If the arrangement should be revealed, the company stood to lose considerable prestige in the eyes of the Latin American people, but Trippe took this chance. Pan American negotiated for the land through its own administrative machinery and was reimbursed for its expenditures by the United States government. The United States, in return, received the right to use the Airport Development Program facilities for ninety-nine years from the contract expiration date.[9]

At first, progress in the building program was disturbingly slow. There were language barriers, a lack of standardization of tools and procedures, disputes on labor policies, poor health of American and native personnel due to the lack of sanitation, slow transportation, and unreliable mail service. One of the most urgent tasks was extending airfield runways and making them capable of bearing the landing pressures of large tactical aircraft. At most sites, facilities were primitive and working conditions disagreeable during the early phases of the project. Fuel had to be stored in steel drums and planes serviced by hand pumps. Mechanics repaired their planes in broiling heat, swirling sandstorms, or drenching rains. Sleeping quarters were practically nonexistent, and many workers slept in the aircraft. During 1942, the submarine menace hindered the building project because many ships bearing needed materials were sunk in the Caribbean or off the coast of South America.[10]

Other events, less spectacular than the sinkings by submarines, were a part of the day-by-day drama of strengthening the Caribbean and adjacent areas. Typical of these events was the fate of a United States Army officer, an enlisted man, and their guides, who were on a jungle-surveying mission. Indians, evidently frightened by their motor-driven canoe, shot two arrows into the officer's chest. After falling overboard, he was pierced again in the back of the neck and soon disappeared in the murky water. The enlisted man drowned, and three of the guides were lost. Their bodies presumably were eaten by fish, but portions of their skeletons were identified later.[11]

The early successes of German Field Marshall Erwin Rommel in Africa convinced President Roosevelt and Secretary of War Henry L. Stimson that thousands of troops and many tons of supplies would be required to stop him. By 1940, Germany possessed several types of aircraft with ranges that permitted operations across the Atlantic. Three presented especially serious threats to the Caribbean area: the Heinkel 111-K, with a range of 2,140 miles; the Focke-Wulf 200, with a range of 3,000 miles; and the Heinkel 177, with a range of 3,400 miles.[12] The president became increasingly concerned about the safety of the Panama Canal.

Military planners realized that, to protect the Caribbean area adequately, adjacent territories would have to be strengthened—particularly the vulnerable "bulge" of Brazil. An aerial "bridge" would have to be erected from Florida to Brazil and from there to Africa, to carry troops and supplies. The southern route was longer than the one across the North Atlantic, but several factors favored its use. There was year-round suitable weather for flying, and the southern route lay over two great land masses. In addition, the Antilles chain formed excellent stepping stones from Miami to the Guianas.

In November 1940, the War Plans Division of the War Department indicated that it would assign top priority to the completion of facilities in the Caribbean. Early the next year the War Department decided to detail Army Air Corps officers for flight duty with Pan American Airways in order to familiarize them with the Caribbean area and with transoceanic conditions generally. Several obstacles had to be overcome, however. One was a ruling by the Judge Advocate General in December 1939 that officers of the regular army could not be detailed as members of commercial carrier crews.[13]

The project personnel refused to be stopped by any such legalistic rulings. Pan American proposed a nine-month training program for army pilots who had two hundred hours of flying time and were otherwise acceptable to company officials. The course included from one to two months of preliminary familiarization with routine procedures, with subsequent assignment as first officers of Pan American transports in regular operation over Caribbean routes. The company would furnish regular Pan American uniforms to be worn by all officers in training with their aircraft.[14]

Many hours and thousands of dollars were spent working out details of this plan, but it was never activated. Too many key people on the Army Air Corps staff objected to the arrangement, arguing that costs would far exceed the benefits and that the plan failed to solve the main problem of relieving the pilot shortage. Because of these objections and a lack of Air Corps funds, the plan was dropped in May 1941.[15] Military men involved closely with all aspects of this problem refused to give up, however. They knew that the visual flight conditions over which short-range aircraft would have to operate required an intimate knowledge of landing fields, radio aids to navigation, and weather conditions. They also knew that the quickest and most practical way that army pilots could gain this knowledge would be to fly with seasoned Pan American crewmen.[16]

Pan American attempted to circumvent the obstacles by offering to carry a limited number of "observers" on trips specified by the army at a reduction of forty-five per cent from published tariffs. The airline believed this would satisfy those who feared diplomatic and technical complications, and at the same time would accomplish the original purpose. Pan American was right. The State Department communicated with United States diplomatic representatives in certain Central and South American countries in the summer of 1941 and received assurance that no diplomatic objections to the proposed flights were anticipated. The secretary of war accordingly directed the Chief of Staff of the Army Air Corps to work out required arrangements with Pan American. After the personnel were selected, General Andrews proceeded to implement the project.[17]

In spite of this accomplishment, Secretary Stimson reemphasized the need for increased transport service in the Caribbean and South Atlantic areas. In August 1941, Pan American consummated contracts with certain affiliated companies to establish transport and ferrying services across the Caribbean to South America and Africa. An essential element in the negotiations was an agreement on the part of the United States Army to turn over possession of ten DC-3 and two Lockheed "Lodestar" airplanes to Pan American. This action, in keeping with Secretary Stimson's wishes, made possible increased transport operations.[18] The stepped-up activity in the Caribbean was quite fortunate in view of the Japanese attack on Pearl Harbor in December 1941 and the subsequent total involvement of the United States in war with the Axis powers.

Pan American had grown so large by the end of 1941 that it had to split its activities into several divisions. It organized a number of subsidiaries that operated as distinct entities, such as the Airport Development Program and Pan American Air Ferries. In addition to the giant Pan American system, there were three smaller airlines operating in the Caribbean area and beyond. Eastern Airlines flew its Military Transport Division as far south as Natal, Brazil; Transcontinental and Western Air began their Caribbean operations shortly after the attack on Pearl Harbor; and at the same time American Airlines started scheduled and unscheduled runs across the Caribbean.[19]

Brig. Gen. Robert Olds, commander of the Air Ferrying Command, established in May 1941, traveled throughout the Caribbean and South American areas early in 1942. The army assigned him the mission of surveying facilities and smoothing out various details of Latin American-United States relations. Specifically, he was to become acquainted with such key people as Gen. Eduardo Gomes, commander of Brazil's air arm. Olds knew that the contribution of the Caribbean countries to the Allied war effort depended largely on how much United States activity Brazil would allow in her country. Upon completion of his trip, General Olds invited Gomes to return with him for a visit in the nation's capital. Olds informed army headquarters that he believed it would be psychologically advantageous for certain equipment to be delivered to his distinguished guest while he was in Washington.[20]

The army arranged for a mammoth ceremony of welcome for the two generals when they arrived at Bolling Field, Maryland, in March 1942. Through this action the United States hoped to impress all of Latin America with the sincerity of its war effort. Gomes was accorded every courtesy, including a motorcycle police escort to near-royal accommodations at one of Washington's finest hotels. When General Gomes returned to Bolling Field to depart for home, he found six P-40 pursuit planes and six twin-engine B-25 "Mitchell" bombers, a part of the fifty aircraft promised to his country, lined up for inspection. The Olds-Gomes association paid high dividends in strengthening United States efforts in Brazil and throughout the Caribbean.[21]

Transport aircraft were vital to the war effort at most Caribbean bases. To meet demands of the military, the commercial lines sacrificed equipment, revised schedules, and shifted personnel without hesitation. Pan American Airways was the largest contract carrier operating across the Caribbean. Its four-engine C-87's, which were converted B-24 bombers designed to carry cargo, participated in more flights than any other aircraft, with the C-47 a close second. By reason of the large number of missions flown, accidents were to be expected in both military and commercial flights. They were especially numerous during the winter of 1942-1943. Operations personnel listed the primary causes as (1) inexperienced pilots, (2) overloading or improper loading, (3) bad weather, and (4) maintenance difficulties.[22]

As one means of improving flying safety and, at the same time, increasing the security of the entire Caribbean, the United States gave top priority to developing the Army Airways Communication System (AACS). Operating initially at Atkinson Field, near Georgetown, British Guiana, AACS was essential to successful air operations and to the defense of the entire Caribbean area. The main mission of AACS was to guide aircraft by radio and to help identify friend or foe. It did this by transmitting information concerning the movement of aircraft, providing navigational aids, speeding weather data, and generally protecting the pilot and his plane along the entire distance of his flight. AACS specialists enabled pilots to fly on instruments around the globe and to land safely under weather conditions that otherwise would have meant almost certain death.

AACS expanded from Atkinson to other areas in the Caribbean and down the Brazilian coast toward its bulge as the war continued. The War Department suspected that the Germans had built several airports inland in South America by transporting supplies by submarine.[23] By August 1942, AACS had multiplied its stations in Central and South America. Living under primitive conditions, members of that organization spent years without furloughs, hewing paths through the jungles, setting up facilities, and operating units.

Both Latin American and United States military commanders were constantly concerned about the problem of security. In most Latin American countries there were large numbers of Germans, Japanese, and Italians. The Germans had trained the Brazilian army, and one of Brazil's top military officials had received several German decorations. United States officials suspected the Italian airline LATI of having taken aerial photographs before the war, which they believed aided Axis submarines in sinking Allied shipping in the Caribbean and South Atlantic waters.[24] Most areas were endangered by surprise hit-and-run attacks, sabotage, commando sorties, and shelling from submarines or other ocean raiders that could come in close to shore or up a river. During the early years of the war, only obsolete interceptor aircraft were available for air defense; and, because of maintenance troubles, most of these machines spent much of the time on the ground. Consequently, air defense was confined largely to patrols, with B-25's and Lockheed "Hudsons" on the short runs, and four-engine B-24 "Liberators" on the longer ones. These bomber aircraft, however, had been designed neither for interception nor patrol.[25]

As operations increased, so did the problems. The questions of the speed of movement, amount of traffic, and safety were subjects of some outstanding controversies between civilian and military officials. The commercial carriers, with their habitual emphasis on absolute safety, were reluctant to make night landings in some areas of the Caribbean. The army believed that getting critical supply items through to the combat forces in a hurry was worth the risk. Long hops expedited the movement of cargo and passengers, but made it necessary to carry more fuel and smaller loads. Everyone concerned wrestled with the perpetual problem of increasing the critical load of the planes to the maximum that was consistent with safety.[26]

The spring of 1942 was a critical period, with all air bases crowded and supplies running low. Allied commanders badly needed a more effective system of priorities. Commercial airlines handled all shipments chronologically, subject to occasional special orders and to the space available on outbound planes. Since some cargo was backlogged for more than a month, this procedure meant that a box marked for Gen. Claire Chennault in China or British Gen. Sir Claude Auchinleck in the Middle East would have to wait its turn. The situation was relieved in May by the formation of the South Atlantic wing of the Air Transport Command, a significant milestone in World War II military aviation. In August the ninth and tenth Ferrying Groups came into existence.[27]

When the African conflict began in November 1942, traffic across the Caribbean multiplied fantastically, particularly that involving munitions en route from the United States to Cairo. A news release at the time reported that these shipments, more than any other kind of support, enabled Great Britain's Lt. Gen. Bernard L. Montgomery to hold his position at El Alamein, a battle that possibly altered the entire course of the war.[28] At the same time, the Caribbean witnessed a mammoth movement of supplies northward by both air and sea transport. As a result of the recommendations of the Board of Economic Warfare, United States contractors began buying large quantities of vital raw materials, such as mica, quartz, and beryllium, from Latin America.[29]

With the shift of warfare in Africa from defensive to offensive, the logistics assumed even greater importance. Enemy submarines sank large numbers of ships in the Atlantic and Caribbean in the fall of 1942, making the movement of materials and men by water slow and dangerous. In December the air route across the North Atlantic was closed for the winter. Virtually all air traffic to Europe and Africa, a large percentage of the planes and supplies for India and China, and some of the lend-lease materials to Russia were routed across the Caribbean to South America.[30]

In early 1943, operations officers feverishly pressed every available plane into service. They converted B-24's into long-range transports by removing some of the fuel tanks to make room for cargo desperately needed in Africa. Operations officers also established rigid priorities, arranged for the handling of VIP's, and screened the numerous requests for special favors from British, French, United States, and Latin American civilian groups.[31]

As the tempo of the war increased, most Latin American countries cooperated closely with the United States in tightening their defenses. This was particularly true of Panama because of the fear of sabotage by submarine-borne troops. Interceptor aircraft were pressed into service as soon as they rolled off the assembly line and were placed under the control of the various theater commanders. Types of equipment in the interceptor inventory included pursuit aircraft, all-weather planes, antiaircraft artillery, and barrage balloons. The Army Air Force assisted the Marine Corps in moving troops to Panama and other vital areas, where they were dispersed to protect such critical targets as airfields, troop encampments, and warehouses.

Many thousands of pounds of freight continued to pile up at Miami warehouses awaiting shipment. It was all emergency equipment, such as aircraft engines, bound for the combat forces in Africa. Desert operations there reduced the life of the Allison and Wright engines to an average of only forty hours—a fraction of what could be expected in normal conditions. Commercial airlines could not meet the pressure put upon them; the furious fighting was gobbling up supplies too fast. The new wing of the South Atlantic had a clearly defined mission. Operations officers not only would have to set up meaningful priorities and obtain more freight aircraft, but they would also have to insure that planes carry more than ever before. Air commanders, in addition, would be required to reduce the number of aircraft accidents, which were beginning to have an adverse psychological affect on the flying personnel. Some of the problems were lessened by reorganization and by acquisition of improved charts for air navigation.[32]

The rapidly expanding war so diversified aerial operations that they raced ahead of supporting facilities, even of navigation charts. The available charts were quite inadequate in 1942, and the army urged that the shoreline from French Guiana southward be completely photographed. Existing maps at the time were so inaccurate that to follow them would mean heavy loss of aircraft—particularly the pursuit type. In the fall of 1942, the third and fourth Photo Mapping Squadrons began taking pictures of the entire triangle of the South American continent from Panama to Rio de Janeiro. At the same time, commanders considerably improved pilot briefings. These measures noticeably reduced aircraft accidents and provided accurate information of a general nature about the area.[33]

The tasks of personnel operating in the Caribbean were as varied as the types of cargo their planes carried. An example is the case of a major of the Iraqi Army, who flew across the Caribbean on a military aircraft in August 1943 bound for the United States. He wore a wooden leg and carried a spare in his luggage. In changing planes at one of the bases, he lost his spare, and a minor international incident was in the making. Lengthy correspondence and an exhaustive search followed. A clerk at last found the leg wrapped in burlap partially hidden under supplies in a dark corner of one of the terminals. It was dispatched northward at once, and Washington commended Air Transport Command for a job well done.[34]

As more army pilots were trained and pressed into service, they relieved Pan American of flying many missions that were of a military nature. While traffic was at its peak, there came a dramatic change in support services. The Airport Development Program, the elaborate dodge concealed as a Pan American subsidiary, by which the United States built military bases throughout the Caribbean and South America, came to an end on June 30, 1944. It had served its purpose well, but the army engineers took over its functions. Pan American Airways, operating in a unique capacity as part military and part civilian, part builders and part flyers, unquestionably provided a valuable service to hemisphere security in those critical times.

Air Transport Command headquarters proposed to the War Department in August 1944 that the Caribbean Division and the South Atlantic Division be merged. Responsible personnel wanted the long chain of bases from Florida to Africa to be placed under a single commander. In effect this would have made the Caribbean the very center of air operations in the hemisphere. But vigorous objections voiced by military representatives in Brazil forced abandonment of the plan.[35]

In the spring of 1945, the Mexican Air Force was strengthened by shipments of B-25 medium bombers from the United States. Mexico earlier had been considered eligible to receive a number of A-20's, light bombers that had proved to be quite popular and versatile. Military planners, however, decided that the B-25 was easier to operate and maintain. They reasoned further that it had the advantage of dual controls and would provide training for a considerably larger number of crew members at the same cost as that of the A-20. The War Department, however, decided that in the future no other Latin American country would be considered for any medium bombers because of State Department objections and other complications.[36]

The unconditional surrender of Germany in May 1945 left the Caribbean countries that had committed themselves to the war in a difficult position. For them the war was over, but their friend and ally, the United States, was still at war with Japan. Gen. Henry H. Arnold, Chief of the Air Force, made a detailed tour of all Caribbean bases the same month. He sensed a need to secure an agreement whereby the United States might continue to use strategic areas there until the war in the Pacific was concluded.[37] This had been one of President Roosevelt's primary concerns, and he had planned to be involved personally in the negotiations. But unlike the war in Europe, which seemed to pose a serious threat, the Pacific conflict caused little personal or national concern in the Caribbean countries. The people seemed ready to address themselves to matters peculiarly their own and leave the complexities of international affairs to others.[38]

Taken as a whole, the extensive teamwork in the Caribbean, developed at a time when the United States was suffering serious military setbacks, represented an accomplishment of great magnitude. Many of its features were transitory, but others were of permanent value. The United States and the Caribbean countries had welded together an American front to resist the attacks of European and Asiatic totalitarianism against this hemisphere. Beyond any doubt, the Caribbean became the crossroads of the free world, and the Caribbean peoples demonstrated, for the most part, that the creed of the Good Neighbor was more than a slogan.

Notes

1. Mark S. Watson, *United States Army in World War II—Chief of Staff: Prewar Plans and Preparations* (Washington: Historical Division, Department of the Army, 1950), p. 94.

2. U. S., Department of State, "Construction of a Ship Canal to Connect Waters of the Atlantic and Pacific Oceans," Treaty Series, no. 431 (Washington, D. C., 1938).

3. Samuel I. Rosenman, *The Public Papers and Addresses of Franklin D. Roosevelt* (New York: Random House, 1941), pp. 392–394.

4. Ibid.

5. "The Army Air Force in World War II," *Air Corps News Letter* (June 1, 1941, Washington, D.C.), vol. 24, no. 11. [No authors are indicated for many articles in this publication.]

6. "Acquisition of Air Bases in Latin America, June 1939–June 1943," U.S. Historical Archives, Maxwell Air Force Base, Alabama, *United States Air Force Historical Study Number 63*, pp. 121–122. [No authors are indicated for most of these studies prepared for the United States Air Force.]

7. Ibid.

8. "War Department Corps of Engineers Historical Study, Final Project Report," Airport Development Program, U.S. Historical Archives, Maxwell Air Force Base, Alabama, pp. 32–33.

9. "Acquisition of Air Bases in Latin America," p. 151.

10. *History of Ibura Field*, U.S. Historical Archives, Maxwell Air Force Base, Alabama, pp. 50–55.

11. *The Official History of the South Atlantic Division, Air Transport Command* (7 pts.), U.S. Historical Archives, Maxwell Air Force Base, Alabama, pt. 5, pp. 34–35.

12. Col. H. L. George, Assistant Chief of Air Staff, to Chief of Air Staff, Jan. 7, 1942, U.S. Historical Archives, Maxwell Air Force Base, Alabama.

13. War Department memorandum to Gen. Carl A. Spaatz, Pan American Airways files, U.S. Historical Archives, Maxwell Air Force Base, Alabama.

14. Undated conference notes, Pan American Airways files, U.S. Historical Archives, Maxwell Air Force Base, Alabama.

15. Gen. George H. Brett memorandum, Plans Division, War Department, to Pan American Airways Planning Committee, May 6, 1941, Pan American Airways files, U.S. Historical Archives, Maxwell Air Force Base, Alabama.

16. Undated conference notes, Pan American Airways files, U.S. Historical Archives, Maxwell Air Force Base, Alabama.

17. Henry L. Stimson to Chief of Army Air Corps, June 4, 1941, Pan American Airways files, U.S. Historical Archives, Maxwell Air Force Base, Alabama.

18. Harlee Branch of the Civil Aeronautics Board, to the Secretary of War, Sept. 13, 1941, Pan American Airways, Airport Development Program Files, New York Office.

19. *The Official History of the South Atlantic Division, Air Transport Command,* pt. 2, p. 132.

20. Ibid., pt. 1, p. 135.

21. Ibid.

22. *History of Parnamirim Field,* U.S. Historical Archives, Maxwell Air Force Base, Alabama, p. 152.

23. *Army Airways Communication Service Historical Data,* Folder no. 383, pp. 1–156, U.S. Historical Archives, Maxwell Air Force Base, Alabama.

24. Harold Sims, United States vice-consul in Natal, to Jefferson Caffery, United States ambassador to Brazil, Mar. 20, 1942, U.S. Historical Archives, Maxwell Air Force Base, Alabama.

25. *The Official History of the South Atlantic Division,* pt. 2, p. 116.

26. Ibid., p. 138.

27. South Atlantic Wing General Order no. 3, Aug. 18, 1942, U.S. Historical Archives, Maxwell Air Force Base, Alabama.

28. United States news release, Natal, Aug. 2, 1942, by Alan Coogan, U.S. Historical Archives, Maxwell Air Force Base, Alabama.

29. *The Official History of the South Atlantic Division,* pt. 3, pp. 1–3.

30. Ibid.

31. Gordon Lethem, Georgetown, British Guiana, to Brig. Gen. R. L. Walsh, Nov. 10, 1942, U.S. Historical Archives, Maxwell Air Force Base, Alabama.

32. "Briefing in the South Atlantic Division of the Air Transport Command," *Historical Records Report, January 1942–November 1944* (file 310–1a), U.S. Historical Archives, Maxwell Air Force Base, Alabama.

33. Ibid.

34. *The Official History of the South Atlantic Division Air Transport Command,* pt. 4, p. 26.

35. Brig. Gen. H. L. George memorandum to Maj. Gen. Ralph H. Wooten, Sept. 16, 1944, U.S. Historical Archives, Maxwell Air Force Base, Alabama.

36. Maj. Gen. R.L. Walsh, U.S. Army, to chief, logistics division, Army Air Force, Subject: "Disposal of A–20 Aircraft," Mar. 9, 1945, U.S. Historical Archives, Maxwell Air Force Base, Alabama.

37. *New York Times,* May 3, 1945.

38. *The Official History of the South Atlantic Division, Air Transport Command,* pt. 7, p. 253.

10 | Congress Investigates Puerto Rico, 1943-1944

Annadrue Brownback

Ponce de León conquered the island of Puerto Rico in 1508, making it one of the earliest European settlements in the New World. Though overshadowed by other regions opened up by the Conquistadores, the island remained under the rule of Spain for almost four centuries—longer than any other American possession of that country. In 1897, as a result of political pressures at home and unrest in Cuba, Spain granted Puerto Rico virtual self-government and the right to send representatives to the Spanish Cortes. The following year, however, the islanders found themselves cut loose from the mother country and welcomed troops from the United States as their liberators. Their hopes for self-rule were frustrated when they discovered that they were to be granted substantially less autonomy by their American liberators than they had enjoyed under the Spanish.

The first civilian government in Puerto Rico under United States control was established in 1900. The executive branch was headed by a governor appointed by the President of the United States. The Puerto Ricans were granted only partial control of the legislative branch of their government. For any changes in their political status, the islanders were dependent on the two United States congressional committees on territories, which were largely responsible for legislation pertaining to Puerto Rico. Congressmen in Washington were rarely unfriendly to the Puerto Ricans, but they were so preoccupied with affairs of their own constituencies that they did not give much time or thought to the island's problems. Residents of the territory, without the vote to command the attention of politicians, found themselves without effective representation in Congress.

Between 1900 and 1943, measures were taken to grant more self-government to the territory. Both houses of the legislature were made elective, and many appointments required the approval of the Puerto Rican Senate. During World War II, however, the wartime restrictions and shortages aggravated the chronic poverty of the island and produced a state of unrest. The many Puerto Ricans serving in the United States armed forces were bitterly aware of their status as second-class citizens. From the dissatisfaction emerged an insistent demand for changes in the political status of the territory. Many citizens wanted to elect their own governor rather than have him appointed by the President of the United States. There was widespread disagreement among Puerto Ricans, however, regarding the exact kind of government that would be best for the island.

For forty years before World War II, the island's politics were characterized by a contest between factions. The Republican Party of Puerto Rico, allied with its mainland counterpart, worked to have the territory admitted as a state. On the other hand, several political parties shared the hope for complete independence. A major turning point came in 1940 when the Popular Democrats, led by Luis Muñoz Marín, won a slim majority in the legislature.[1] Previously, many members of this Party had worked for independence. At the time of the victory, however, its leaders offered a new approach: they merely stated that they would strive to improve economic and social conditions on the island. Continuing this pragmatic outlook, by 1943 several Popular Democrats were convinced that Puerto Rico needed some sort of autonomous government, but one within the tariff wall of the United States. With cooperation from Territorial Governor Rexford G. Tugwell, they launched "Operation Bootstrap," an economic development program based on the existing financial relationship between Puerto Rico and the United States.

Other factions on the island disagreed with the Popular Democrats. The Republican Party continued to support statehood as the best solution, saying that in no other way could Puerto Ricans be guaranteed the same freedom to manage their own affairs as that enjoyed by other United States citizens. They recognized that statehood would entail certain economic hardships.[2] However, they felt that, with the stability and dignity of a state government, plus representation in Congress, Puerto Rico could soon overcome its economic problems. At the other extreme, the *independentistas*, some of whom were in the Popular Democratic Party, felt that no solution short of complete independence would allow Puerto Ricans to govern themselves as a free people.

Accusations of mismanagement, dishonesty, Communism, and other improprieties were directed at the government of the Popular Democrats. Some of these charges reached the ear of Senator Harry S. Truman; and, partly because of his insistence, the Senate Committee on Territories and Insular Affairs decided to look carefully into Puerto Rican Affairs.[3] The Senate authorized the formation of a subcommittee to investigate social and economic conditions on the island. In spite of the limited authorization, many of the hearings were actually concerned with political conditions in Puerto Rico. Islanders of various political persuasions, realizing that the final determination of their status would have to come from Congress, bent their efforts toward persuading the committee that their particular solutions were the best ones. After completing its investigation, the committee was convinced that the Puerto Rican situation was a critical one. In its final report the committee concluded: "Radical changes and appropriate overhauling of the governmental machinery controlling island–United States relations are indispensable." [4]

The report of the Senate subcommittee did not have any immediate results. In fact, owing to the pressures of the war and other urgent matters, no major changes in the status of Puerto Rico came before 1945. However, in 1943 and 1944, four additional hearings were conducted by committees of the Seventy-eighth Congress.

Before the Senate group finished its hearings, a subcommittee of the House Committee on Insular Affairs began a second investigation, designed to review political, economic, and social conditions in Puerto Rico. Chairman C. Jasper Bell of Missouri and his subcommittee conducted hearings that resulted in 1,680 pages of testimony and 774 pages of appendices, charts, and special information of various sorts.[5] In spite of its length, the report of the Bell Committee's investigation was of little value. Investigators failed to bring out all sides of the issues, but concentrated on information that would discredit Muñoz Marín, the Popular Democrats, or the New Deal appointee, Governor Rexford Tugwell.[6]

The third congressional investigation was conducted in 1943 in connection with a bill designed to limit the term of office for the governor of Puerto Rico. This proposal was the work of Bolívar Pagán, the Puerto Rican resident commissioner, and was designed primarily to undermine the Muñoz-Tugwell regime. Throughout the hearings, Pagán and other members of the committee continued to attack Tugwell and his policies.[7] With the completion of the investigation, Pagán's bill, as well as a similar measure introduced in the Senate, failed to pass.

The next congressional hearing was held in May 1943 on an independence bill introduced by Senator Millard Tydings, a Democrat from Maryland. In support of his bill, Senator Tydings emphasized the state of unrest in Puerto Rico, saying that "some Governors down there . . . would hardly dare go on the street." [8] One feature of the bill, a clause stating that none of its provisions should take effect without Puerto Rican approval, pleased the islanders.[9] Both in Washington and in Puerto Rico, however, opponents attacked the measure on a number of grounds. John J. McCloy, assistant secretary of war, speaking on behalf of his department, urged that no action on Puerto Rican independence be considered until after the war. Senator Robert A. Taft took the same position, feeling that Senator Tydings had exaggerated the state of unrest in the territory.[10]

During the hearings on independence, some interesting attitudes of individual investigators were revealed. Several senators were indignant to find that Puerto Rican schoolchildren could not speak English. Their indignation increased when some Puerto Rican leaders expressed the opinion that a knowledge of the English language was not essential in the light of the undetermined political status of their island. Some committee members considered the expressed desire of Puerto Ricans for freedom tantamount to treason, yet the hearing in which they were participating was related to a congressional bill providing for the island's independence. Furthermore, Puerto Rican witnesses had been told that they should not hope for statehood, because Congress would never grant it. Thus their only choice seemed to be between independence and continued colonialism. It was an extraordinarily ambivalent attitude that allowed Americans to discuss the possibility of Puerto Rican independence but brand the islanders' hopes of freedom as treason.

On March 9, 1943, President Roosevelt asked Congress to consider an amendment to the Organic Act, "to permit the people of Puerto Rico to elect their own governor, and to redefine the functions and powers of the federal government and the government of Puerto Rico, respectively." [11] At the same time, the president appointed a committee to suggest to him appropriate changes in the Organic Act. Members of this committee were Secretary of the Interior Harold Ickes, Undersecretary of the Interior Abe Fortas, Governor Rexford Tugwell, Father Raymond A. McGowan, Luis Muñoz

Marín, Judge Martin Travieso, Celestino Iriarte, and José Ramírez-Santibañez. Each of the Puerto Rican members was the head of a political party, except Judge Travieso, who was supposed to be impartial. No member of the United States Congress was appointed, but out of this committee's proposals was to come the fifth and most significant of the congressional hearings relating to the future political status of Puerto Rico.

The president's committee began its meetings on July 19, 1943. After the first session, Abe Fortas acted as chairman and B. W. Thoron, also of the Department of the Interior, served as an alternate in place of Secretary Ickes.[12] Muñoz Marín attended rather reluctantly because he felt uneasy about making recommendations for any changes in the Organic Act that did not include the machinery for determining the final political status of his island.[13] He felt that if Congress passed a bill providing for an elected governor, it would be very difficult to get consideration for additional changes in the Puerto Rican government for a long time. The other Puerto Rican members of the committee agreed with Muñoz Marín on this point.[14] In the matter of an elected governor, however, the proceedings in the committee went smoothly. The acceptance was a foregone conclusion—it was what the president had requested, and all the members of the committee favored it.

The first real difficulty arose over the question of a representative of the United States Government in Puerto Rico. Major differences appeared between the ideas of the islanders and those of the continentals. Judge Travieso expressed his opinion in the following terms:

> If I had the choice, and if it depended on my own personal vote, I would rather have the island continue the present system as it is now than to have a high commissioner with all the powers appertaining to an English high commissioner and a governor that would be merely a sort of high-class mayor of our community, to administer local affairs and to take a secondary place in the official functions and everything else, where the high commissioner would be over him.[15]

The other Puerto Rican members were in complete accord with Travieso's statement and insisted that an elected governor should have all the duties, responsibilities, privileges, and honors which the appointed governors had always had. The continental committeemen felt that there was a decided difference between a governor who, as a presidential appointee, represented the federal government directly, and an elected official who would represent the people of Puerto Rico.

Muñoz continued to express concern over the possibility that early congressional action on a bill providing for an elected governor would preclude action on other measures relating to the future status of Puerto Rico. He suggested that the bill relating to the elective governorship should also include a provision for a constitutional convention or a plebiscite.[16] Tugwell felt that a convention or plebiscite would produce unfortunate results unless it were conducted within clearly defined limits. He wanted, of course, to prevent the Puerto Ricans from choosing a status that Congress was not prepared to grant them. Fortas felt that any recommendation about a constitutional convention or plebiscite would exceed the instructions from the President.[17]

Puerto Rican Senator Celestino Iriarte joined Muñoz Marín in calling for a commitment on the permanent status of their island. He pointed out that it was a little embarrassing for loyal Americans in Puerto Rico to have some United States congressman introduce a bill granting unrequested and unwanted independence to the territory. Iriarte contended that Puerto Rican statehood was the only permanent solution.[18] When Muñoz Marín objected to this viewpoint, Iriarte challenged him to name an acceptable alternative. With characteristic disregard for tradition and precedent, the leader of the Popular Democratic Party replied, "Oh, we could invent some." [19] At that point Governor Tugwell hinted at a solution that would later be followed when he asked, "Are Canadians citizens of the British Commonwealth?" [20] Muñoz pointed out that forty-five years earlier the Spaniards had granted a charter to Puerto Rico, which not only gave the island an autonomous form of government but also provided that amendments to the charter should be made only on the initiative of the Puerto Rican government. He strongly suggested that the United States should do no less.[21] Members of the committee were aware that there was a rather general feeling of resentment in Puerto Rico concerning the power of Congress to change the Organic Act of the territory without any reference whatever to the wishes of the citizens.

The power of Congress to make changes in Puerto Rico's government was especially distasteful to the Popular Democrats at that time. Two bills then pending in the Seventy-eighth Congress, if enacted into law, would have brought to an immediate halt the economic progress being made under Operation Bootstrap. The first provided for rum revenues collected in Puerto Rico to be placed in the United States treasury to be appropriated by Congress for Puerto Rican welfare. The second bill called for the annulment of the entire body of laws on which Operation Bootstrap was based, including those establishing the Water Resources Authority and the Transportation Authority.[22] Indicating his feeling regarding the ability of Congress to superimpose its authority over Puerto Rican programs, Muñoz Marín suggested that Congress had forgotten that one more law should be annulled—the law allowing Puerto Ricans to vote.[23] Governor Tugwell made an interesting reference to the other side of the picture, saying that the power of Congress to change Puerto Rico's Organic Act had not "in practice, proved dangerous." On the contrary, the failure of Congress to act at all, leaving the island with unchanged governmental machinery in a rapidly changing world, had been a much more serious matter.[24]

Abe Fortas believed that in looking for permanence the Puerto Ricans were chasing a "will-o'-the-wisp." [25] He felt very strongly that the insertion of any such provision in the Elected Governor Bill would greatly endanger the passage of the entire measure. While he saw Muñoz Marín's point, he favored the "bird in the hand" theory, and advised accepting the bill, if it could be obtained, and then going on for other things.[26] He thought a good solution might be to incorporate in the committee's recommendation a proposal for a joint committee to study the status of Puerto Rico and to report to Congress.[27] Muñoz was not much impressed with this suggestion, feeling that a constitutional convention in Puerto Rico would do a better job of studying and recommending changes in its status. Fortas opposed a convention on the same grounds that Tugwell had cited: he felt that it would be very bad for morale in the territory if, for example, the convention chose statehood, and Congress rejected their proposal.[28]

The bill which the committee finally drafted to amend the Puerto Rican Organic Act was full of compromises—not completely satisfactory to anyone but at least acceptable to all. The bill provided for an elected governor, a commissioner general to represent the interests of the federal government in Puerto Rico, increased power and responsibilities for the territorial legislature, and other minor changes. The question of permanence was covered by a provision stating that it was the intention of Congress that further changes in the bill should be made only with the consent of Puerto Rico. This draft was introduced in the Senate on October 1, 1943 and was known as S. 1407.[29]

In the Senate, the bill was referred to a subcommittee of the Committee of Territories and Insular Affairs and public hearings were begun.[30] In the course of the hearings, various congressmen and Puerto Rican leaders expressed their attitudes toward autonomous government for Puerto Rico. An early objection to the proposed law was that it apparently made an effort to tie the hands of future Congresses by expressing the intention that further changes in the Organic Act would be made only with the consent of Puerto Rico. Senators Ralph O. Brewster and Robert A. Taft registered objections to this provision.[31] Senator Allen J. Ellender agreed with the Puerto Rican members of the committee that had drafted the bill that the office of commissioner general was unnecessary. Ellender added that it would also be costly, and it might provide the islanders with an excuse should they fail in creating their own self-government.[32]

The principal Puerto Rican opponents of S. 1407 to appear before the Senate subcommittee were *independentistas;* in fact, Dr. Sergio S. Peña, vice-president of the Puerto Rican Pro-Independence Congress, suggested that if a referendum were held on status, the *independentistas* would not vote. He insisted that they did not care to go to the polls in a colonial election, and would vote only in a free country.[33] Peña expressed the belief that the economic problems of Puerto Rico were caused by the inability of industry to develop while under a colonial system and subject to continental competition.[34]

One witness to appear before the senators was E. M. Ellsworth, a native of Massachusetts who had lived in Puerto Rico for twenty-five years. Members of the pro-independence Congress had referred to him as an advocate of independence, but Ellsworth's testimony illustrated a somewhat different attitude. He stated:

> There was a time in the history of Puerto Rico when it was pretty much of a crime to speak out about independence, and as an American I couldn't do anything but stand out for the right of people to speak for independence, and I have done that during my years there. . . . But, if you ask me definitely my opinion today, let me say that what is in my mind is some solution that lets the Puerto Rican

people develop their economy in a way that they can better their standard of living, with complete self-government. But if independence means a retrogression of that economy, I am not the one to say, I feel it is too great a responsibility to say, that a person would rather be independent than eat.[35]

Many other residents of the island who had previously supported independence came to question the wisdom of that course of action, especially after the forward-looking economic programs of the *Populares* began to show signs of success.

The ranks of the Popular Democratic Party were split over the proposal for an elected governor. Muñoz Marín, of course, supported the committee's recommendations, but was unable to carry with him all the members of his party. Senator Vicente Géigel-Polanco, the floor leader of the *Populares*, led a faction that denounced the measures as "compromise with colonialism." He set forth his opinion in the following words:

> The problem of sovereignty does not mean obtaining a mere reform of the existing regime, nor the prolongation of a colonial system with more or less generous economic relief, nor the simple concession of an elective governor, nor transitory measures, nor revocable franchises. It means the complete, absolute, permanent and definitive termination of the colony.[36]

Géigel-Polanco, like Sergio Peña of the pro-independence Congress, blamed economic ills on the political subjugation of the island. He pointed specifically to several political factors that were related to economic and social difficulties. These difficulties included free trade between Puerto Rico and the United States, the application of United States custom duties to Puerto Rico's trade with other countries, and the coastwise shipping laws and their application to the territory.[37]

In the Senate, the foremost advocate of independence for Puerto Rico, Senator Millard E. Tydings, agreed with Géigel-Polanco's position, but assured all Puerto Rican supporters of independence that S. 1407 was "no bar to independence, but . . . simply a step on the road to complete self-government and independence for Puerto Ricans." [38] However, just as some of the former *independentistas* of the island were beginning to recognize that independence was not the best solution for Puerto Rico, so were some members of Congress beginning to realize that a gracious grant of independence by the United States would be anything but a kindness to the territory.

Senator Robert Taft said that the United States could not discharge its responsibility toward Puerto Rico by giving it independence.[39] Taft favored what he called "autonomous dependence" rather than complete independence. This, he said, would "leave the entire government independent, except, say, in diplomatic negotiations and . . . military matters." [40]

When the Senate committee finally did report on the bill, its report was favorable, but the bill had been so changed that it bore little resemblance to the original draft that had been presented by the president's committee. The Senate bill provided for changing the Organic Act chiefly by adding an elected governor, but omitted virtually all other features granting increased autonomy. The Senate committee had struck out the provision declaring it to be the "intention of Congress that no further changes in the Organic Act shall be made except with the concurrence of the people of Puerto Rico or their duly elected representatives," saying that it was "elementary" that Congress could not bind future Congresses.[41] To many Puerto Ricans this was the root of the matter. They felt that without this assurance they would be unable to plan and work for their own improvement with any confidence. They would never know when a legislative blow would fall which would affect their economic situation, cut their production quotas, withhold projected revenues, or make other significant changes.

The Senate debate on the Elected Governor Bill began on February 15, 1944. The provisions of the measure, with the committee's recommendations, were considered one by one. Regarding the committee's decision to strike out the provision that no changes would be made without the consent of Puerto Rico, there was no discussion at all. Apparently, the Senate was in complete accord with the committee on that point.[42] On other portions of the bill, however, objections were raised, reflecting a considerable amount of congressional distrust of the liberal elements in control in Puerto Rico. Senator Arthur H. Vandenberg opposed the Elected Governor Bill, saying that the older territories of Hawaii and Alaska had no elected governor and he did not understand why Puerto Rico should have a privilege not accorded them. Senator Dennis Chávez countered by commenting that the fact that we were not "doing justice to Alaska and Hawaii should not keep us from doing justice to Puerto Rico." [43] Senator Tydings added that Hawaii had never asked to elect her governor, while Puerto Rico had repeatedly asked for this privilege.[44]

Senator Vandenberg then suggested that a good first step would be for the president to appoint a Puerto Rican as governor, a suggestion that reflected his dislike for Governor Tugwell. After a few other pinpricks from various Senators, the bill was passed with no further discussion.[45]

On February 18, 1944, S. 1407 was referred to the House Committee on Insular Affairs. This committee held hearings on the bill late in the summer of 1944; but, perhaps because they felt they had thoroughly covered the Puerto Rican situation in the Bell Committee investigations, these hearings involved only three witnesses—Abe Fortas of the Department of the Interior and Elmer Ellsworth and Jesús T. Piñero of the Puerto Rican legislature. Neither the committee nor the House of Representatives as a body took any great interest in the matter. The House failed to act on the bill, so that the Seventy-eighth Congress adjourned without passing the legislation.

There was much disappointment in both Puerto Rico and Washington that, after so much discussion, so many hearings, and so much debate, Congress had done nothing significant about the Puerto Rican situation. Even though the efforts of the Seventy-eighth Congress bore no immediate fruit, they did serve a useful purpose by clarifying the problem. A few Congressmen who had felt that we were doing too much for an ungrateful colony began to understand the frustrations of a proud people who were denied full political rights.[46] Puerto Ricans, who for generations had elected officials because they pledged support to independence or to statehood, began to understand that neither of these aspirations would be easily attained; and, if attained, either might prove highly undesirable.[47] The problem was indeed a complex one; there was no easy, simple, or universally acceptable solution. By the end of 1944, largely because of the congressional hearings, this fact was much more generally recognized than it had ever been before. The hearings, furthermore, were stepping stones toward the reforms that were to come in the Truman administration, culminating in the Constitution of 1952, under which the island was granted commonwealth status.

Notes

1. This party gained an absolute majority in the Senate, but a working majority in the House only by the cooperation of a minor party. *U.S. Congressional Record* (79th Cong., 1st sess., 1945), vol. 91, pt. 10, p. A213.

2. The federal government had never imposed taxes on Puerto Rico and had refunded to the island the federal taxes collected there.

3. Such complaints usually reached the ear of someone in Washington; it was said of Puerto Rican politics that no one believed an election was over except the man who won. The loser simply packed his bags and went to Washington to continue the fight.

4. U. S., Congress, Senate, Committee on Territories and Insular Affairs, *Subcommittee Report on Economic and Social Conditions in Puerto Rico* (Report No. 628, 78th Cong., 1st sess., 1943), p. 56.

5. U. S., Congress, House, Subcommittee of the Committee on Insular Affairs, *Hearings Pursuant to H. Res. 159 for an Investigation of Political, Economic and Social Conditions in Puerto Rico* (78th Cong., 1st and 2nd sess., 1943–44), passim.

6. Ibid., p. 165. To the suggestion that Tugwell's ideas of government were alien to any held in the United States, one Congressman commented, "Alien to anything except the New Deal philosophy."

7. U. S., Congress, House, Committee on Insular Affairs, *Hearings on H.R. 784, A Bill to Limit the Term of Office of the Governor of Puerto Rico* (78th Cong., 1st sess., 1943), passim.

8. U.S., Congress, Senate, Committee on Territories and Insular Affairs, *Hearings on S. 952, A Bill to Provide for the Withdrawal of the Sovereignty of the United States Over the Island of Puerto Rico and for the Recognition of its Independence* (78th Cong., 1st sess., 1943), p. 13.

9. Ibid., p. 26.

10. Ibid., p. 13.

11. *U. S. Congressional Record* (78th Cong., 1st sess., 1943), vol. 89, pt. 2, p. 1686. The Organic Act was the basic law established to govern Puerto Rico.

12. A stenographic transcript of the proceedings of the meeting of the committee appears as an appendix to U.S., Congress, Senate, Subcommittee of the Committee on Territories and Insular Affairs, *Hearings on S. 1407, A Bill to Amend the Organic Act of Puerto Rico* (78th Cong., 1st sess., 1943), p. 309.

13. Ibid., p. 310.

14. Ibid., pp. 312–313.

15. Ibid., p. 354.

16. Ibid., p. 491. Muñoz felt that at the time of a convention or plebiscite Congress would have either to approve or disapprove the results, but could not ignore them.

17. Ibid., pp. 491–493.

18. Ibid., p. 493.

19. Ibid., 494.

20. Ibid.

21. Ibid.

22. *U.S. Congressional Record* (78th Cong., 1st sess. 1943), vol. 89, pt. 1, p. 1278.

23. In this statement, Muñoz was quoting a *jíbaro*, or rural Puerto Rican. Until the 1940 election, the *jíbaros* had traditionally supplemented

their tiny incomes by selling their votes and had staunchly refused to vote unless they were paid for it. In the revolutionary campaign of 1940 Muñoz, fighting the sugar and other commercial interests, was without funds. He turned to the *jíbaros* for support, asking them to "lend" him their votes and explaining that they could have justice or $2.00—the "going rate" for a vote—but not both. To everyone's surprise, they supported him and became his most enthusiastic followers. Since 1940, buying votes in Puerto Rico has been virtually unheard of. U.S., Congress, Senate, Subcommittee of the Committee on Territories and Insular Affairs, *Hearings on S. 1407* (78th Cong., 1st sess., 1943), p. 516.

24. Rexford G. Tugwell, *The Stricken Land* (Garden City, N.Y.: Doubleday & Co., 1947), p. 259. Tugwell said: "The possibility of irresponsible Congressional action was a constant source of irritation to insular pride. But what had proved dangerous was the reverse of this: an unsympathetic regard for what was often thought of as an ungrateful ward; Congress had hardly changed the [Organic] Act at all, and year by year it had grown more obsolete."

25. U. S., Congress, House, Subcommittee of the Committee on Insular Affairs, *Hearings Pursuant to H. Res. 159 for an Investigation of Political, Economic and Social Conditions in Puerto Rico* (78th Cong., 1st and 2d sess., 1943–1944), p. 495.

26. Ibid., p. 496.

27. Ibid., p. 499.

28. Ibid., p. 502.

29. Ibid., pp. 106 ff. (text of S. 1407).

30. The members of the subcommittee were Senators Dennis Chávez of New Mexico, chairman; Homer T. Bone of Washington; Allen J. Ellender of Louisiana; John A. Danaher of Connecticut; Robert A. Taft of Ohio; and Ralph O. Brewster of Maine.

31. U. S., Congress, Senate, Subcommittee on Territories and Insular Affairs, *S. 1407 Hearings* (78th Cong., 1st. sess., 1943), pp. 13, 21.

32. Ibid., p. 114.

33. Ibid., p. 192.

34. Ibid., p. 202.

35. Ibid., p. 187.

36. Ibid., p. 291.

37. Ibid., p. 292. Géigel-Polanco also linked corporate latifundia, absenteeism in investments, and financial control of the island by American banks as ills growing out of continental domination.

38. Ibid., p. 160.

39. Ibid., p. 187.

40. Ibid.

41. U.S., Congress, Senate, Committee on Territories and Insular Affairs, *Amending the Organic Act of Puerto Rico: Report No. 659, to Accompany S. 1407* (78th Cong., 2d sess., 1944), p. 1.

42. *U.S. Congressional Record* (78th Cong., 2d sess., 1944), vol. 90, pt. 2, p. 1664.

43. Ibid.

44. Ibid.
45. Ibid.
46. Rexford G. Tugwell, *The Art of Politics, As Practiced by Three Great Americans: Franklin D. Roosevelt, Luis Muñoz Marín and Fiorello H. LaGuardia* (Garden City, N.Y.: Doubleday & Co., 1958), p. 36. Tugwell contended that during World War II, ". . . the principles we professed to be fighting for were very poorly observed in our own dependencies. . . ."
47. Puerto Ricans who for years had clung tenaciously to statehood as the only acceptable status solution must have been impressed by hearing so many different senators and representatives in so many different times and places assure them that statehood was not a possibility in the foreseeable future. It is also doubtful whether any *independentista* could have failed to give consideration to the overwhelming preponderance of economists, both insular and continental, who testified that independence would mean economic ruin for the island.

Appendix

THE PUBLICATIONS OF A. B. THOMAS

Research Publications

Books

Forgotten Frontiers: A Study of the Spanish-Indian Policy of Juan Bautista de Anza, Governor of New Mexico, 1777-1787 (University of Oklahoma Press, Norman, 1932; second edition, Nov. 1969).

After Coronado: Spanish Exploration Northeast of New Mexico, 1696-1727 (University of Oklahoma Press, Norman, 1935; second edition, 1966).

The Plains Indians and New Mexico, 1751-1778 (The University of New Mexico Press, Albuquerque, 1940).

Teodoro de Croix and the Northern Frontier of New Spain, 1776-1783 (University of Oklahoma Press, Norman, 1941; second printing, 1968).

Articles in Historical Journals

"The Massacre of the Villasur Expedition on the Forks of the Platte River," *Nebraska History*, VII (July–September 1924), pp. 68–81.

"Spanish Expeditions in Colorado," *The Colorado Magazine*, I, (November 1924), pp. 289–300. [Reprinted in *The Gold Nugget* Fall 1964, V, No. 3, pp. 3–14.]

"Spanish Exploration of Oklahoma, 1599–1792," *Chronicles of Oklahoma*, VI (June 1928), pp. 186–213.

"The Yellowstone River, James Long and Spanish Reaction to American Intrusions into Spanish Dominions, 1818–1819," *West Texas Year Book* (June 1928), pp. 3–15. [Reprinted in the *New Mexico Historical Review*, IV, April 1929, pp. 164–177.]

"Documents Bearing upon the Northern Frontier of New Mexico, 1818–1819," *New Mexico Historical Review*, IV (April 1929), pp. 146–164.

"San Carlos: A Comanche Pueblo on the Arkansas River, 1787," *The Colorado Magazine*, VI (May 1929).

"An Eighteenth Century Comanche Document," *American Anthropologist*, XXXI (April–June 1929), pp. 289–298.

"An Anonymous Description of New Mexico, 1818," *Southwestern Historical Quarterly*, XXXIII (July 1929), p. 50–74.

"Governor Mendinueta's Proposals for the Defense of New Mexico, 1772–1778," *New Mexico Historical Review*, VI (January 1931), pp. 21–39.

"The First Santa Fe Expedition, 1792–1793," *Chronicles of Oklahoma*, IX (June 1931), pp. 195–208.

"A Description of Sonora in 1772," *The Arizona Historical Review*, V (January 1933), pp. 302–307.

"Spanish Activities in the Lower Mississippi Valley, 1513–1698," *The Louisiana Historical Quarterly*, XXII (October 1939), pp. 1–12.

Chapters in Commemorative and Other Volumes

"Antonio de Bonilla and Spanish Plans for the Defense of New Mexico, 1772–1778," *New Spain and the Anglo-American West*, I (Lancaster, Pennsylvania, 1932), pp. 183–209 [Herbert E. Bolton Commemorative Volumes].

"Anza in Sonora, 1777–1778," *Hispanic American Essays: A Memorial to James Alexander Robertson*. A. Curtis Wilgus, Ed., (University of North Carolina Press, Durham, 1942), Chapter 9.

"The Caudillo in the Caribbean: An Interpretation," *The Caribbean: Its Political Problems*. A. Curtis Wilgus, Ed., (University of Florida Press, Gainesville, 1956), pp. 174–186.

"Spanish Travel in the South, 1527–1750," Part I, *Travels in the Old South, A Bibliography*. Thomas D. Clark, Ed. (University of Oklahoma Press, Norman, 1956).

Research Reports on American Indians

"The Jicarilla Apache Indians, A History—1598–1888," University of Alabama, 1958 (mimeographed), pp. 1–152, in the record of the case of the Jicarilla Apache Tribe v. United States, Docket No. 22A, Indian Claims Commission, Washington, D. C.

"The Mescalero and Chiricahua Apache, 1653–1888," University of Alabama, 1959 (mimeographed), pp. 1–43, in the record of the case of the Mescalero-Chiricahua Apache Tribe v. United States, Docket No. 22B, Indian Claims Commission, Washington, D.C.

"The Yavapai Indians, 1582–1848," University of Alabama, 1959 (mimeographed), pp. 1–24, in the record of the case of the Yavapai Indian Tribe v. United States, Indian Claims Commission, Washington, D. C.

"The Lipan Apache: 1718–1856," University of Alabama, 1959 (mimeographed). Report of the University of New Mexico Mescalero-Chiricahua Land Claims Project, pp. 1–13.

Notes

"Spanish Maps: A Tool for the Study of American Colonial History," *The Journal of the Alabama Academy of Science,* XXXIII, No. 4 (October 1962), pp. 223–224.

"The Western Boundary of the Comanche Indians with Special Reference to the Royce Map in the *18th Annual Report* of the Bureau of American Ethnology," *The Journal of the Alabama Academy of Science,* XXXVI, No. 4 (October 1965), pp. 189–190.

General Works

Latin America: A History. (The Macmillan Company, New York, 1956; second printing, 1962.)

Four chapters: "Latin America: Mexico," "Understanding Argentina," "Brazil: Collossus of the South," "The Latin American Mind," *Patterns for Modern Living, Political Patterns.* Part 2. (The Delphian Society, Chicago, 1949), pp. 359–566.

Contemporary Latin American Studies

"Spanish Liberalism," *The Sooner Magazine,* III, No. 4 (January 1931), University of Oklahoma, pp. 128–129, 142–143.

"New Aspects of the Monroe Doctrine," *The Southwest in International Affairs.* Southern Methodist University (Dallas, Texas, 1936), pp. 106–20.

"Basic Factors in Inter-American Peace," *International Institutions and World Peace.* Southern Methodist University (Dallas, Texas, 1937), pp. 227–246.

"Mexico's New Economics," *Southwest Review,* XXXIII (July 1938), pp. 373–91.

"Petróleo en la Politica Inter-Americana," *America,* III, No. 3 (Havana, Cuba: Sept. 1939).

"Latin America and the Post-War World," *World Affairs,* V. 105,

No. 2 (June 1942), pp. 120–125. [American Peace Society, Washington, D.C.].

"Latin America and World Affairs," *The Delphian Quarterly*, V. 29, No. 3 (July 1946), pp. 2–4, 23. [Publication of the Delphian Society, Chicago, Ill.]

"Postlude: Mexico under Alemán," *The Delphian Quarterly*, V. 36, No. 2 (Spring 1953), pp. 16–19.

"The Return of Vargas," *The Delphian Quarterly*, V. 36, No. 3 (Summer 1953), pp. 23–26.

"Perón's Argentina," *The Delphian Quarterly*, V. 36, No. 4 (Autumn 1953), pp. 28–31.

"Perspective on Revolution," *The Delphian Quarterly*, V. 37, No. 1 (Winter 1954), pp. 1–5.

"The United States and Latin America," *The Delphian Quarterly*, V. 37, No. 2 (Spring 1954), pp. 13–18.

"That Foothold in Guatemala," *The Delphian Quarterly*, V. 37, No. 3 (Summer 1954), pp. 35–38.

"Puerto Rico: Our Moral Outpost," *The Delphian Quarterly*, V. 38, No. 1 (Winter 1955), pp. 19–22, 35.

"Central America's Struggle for Stability," *The Delphian Quarterly*, V. 38, No. 2 (Spring 1955), pp. 15–20, 39.

"U. S. Policy and Latin American Realities," *The Delphian Quarterly*, V. 38, No. 3 (Summer 1955), pp. 23–28.

"Argentina and Brazil: Contrast in Revolutions," *The Delphian Quarterly*, V. 39, No. 2 (Spring 1956), pp. 6–11, 37–38.

"Suez and Panama," *The Delphian Quarterly*, V. 39, No. 2 (Autumn 1956), pp. 1–5, 37–38.

"Problems in Latin America Today," *The Delphian Quarterly*, V. 40, No. 4 (Autumn 1957), pp. 17–23.

"Democracy in Industrializing Latin America," *The Delphian Quarterly*, V. 43, No. 2 (Spring 1960), pp. 27–30, 36.

"Brazil—Problems and Trends," *The Delphian Quarterly*, V. 44, No. 2 (Spring 1961), pp. 11–14, 27–28.

"Frondizi's Problems," *The Delphian Quarterly*, V. 45, No. 1 (Winter 1962), pp. 19–23.

"The Latin American Common Market," *The Delphian Quarterly*, V. 45, No. 2 (Spring 1962), pp. 19–22, 28.

"Latin America, Communism and the Changing World," *Communism and the Changing World*, West Georgia College Studies in the Social Sciences, V. 1, No. 1 (May 1962), pp. 31–41.

"The Federal Executive Council in Uruguay," *The Delphian Quarterly*, V. 45, No. 4 (Autumn 1962), pp. 32–37.

"The Role of the Communists in Chile," *The Delphian Quarterly*, V. 46, No. 3 (Summer 1963), pp. 15–20, 27.

"Latin America: Arms and the Man," *The Delphian Quarterly*, V. 47, No. 2 (Spring 1964), pp. 15–20, 33.

"Education in Latin America," *The Delphian Quarterly*, V. 47, No. 4 (Autumn 1964), pp. 1–6, 29.

"Latin American Nationalism and the United States," *Journal of Inter-American Studies*, VII, No. 1 (January 1965), pp. 5–13.

"Mexico's Changing Economy," *The Delphian Quarterly*, V. 48, No. 2 (Spring 1965), pp. 1–6.

"Latin America's Answer to Communism" (Part I), *The Delphian Quarterly*, V. 49, No. 2 (Spring 1966), pp. 1–3, 22.

"Latin America's Answer to Communism" (Part II), *The Delphian Quarterly*, V. 49, No. 3 (Summer 1966), pp. 8–12.

"Panama in Transition," *The Delphian Quarterly*, V. 49, No. 3 (Summer 1967), pp. 6–10, 18, 22.

"Guatemala Today: What Promise," *The Delphian Quarterly*, V. 50, No. 1 (Winter 1967), pp. 5–10.

Miscellaneous Studies

"Ponce de Leon," and "Hernando de Soto," in the *Encyclopedia Britannica*, 1967.

"A Summary History of the Alumni, 1836–1954," University of Alabama *Alumni Bulletin*, XVIII, No. 1 (Summer 1964), pp. 1–4.

"Understanding Latin America," *Alabama School Journal*, V. 61, No. 6 (February 1944), pp. 5, 13.

"How Our Schools Can Help Us to Understand Latin America," *The County Herald* (The Journal of the Jefferson County Teachers Association, Birmingham, Alabama: March 15, 1962), V. 23, No. 4, p. 8.

"Democracy Struggle: Real Latin American Story" *Birmingham News* (July 16, 1967).

Index

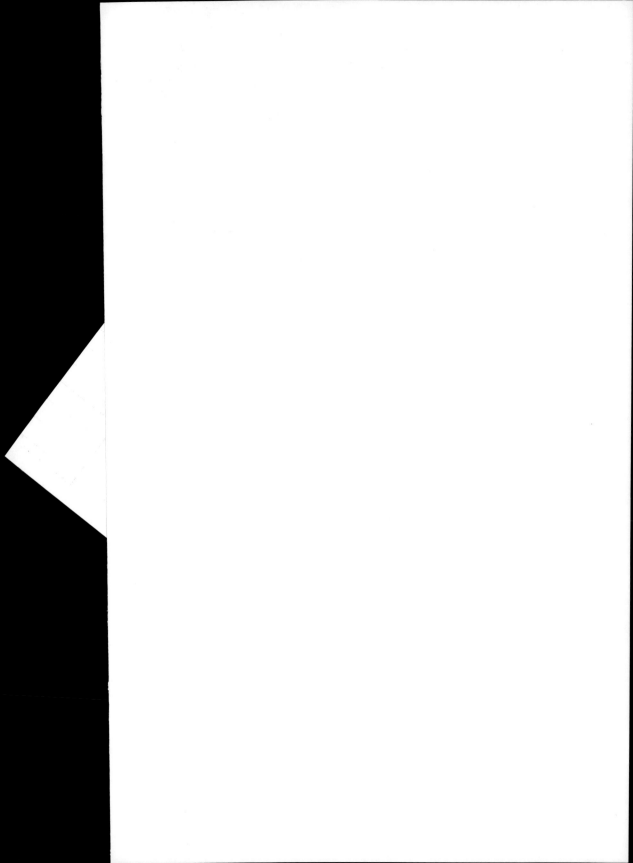

DATE DUE

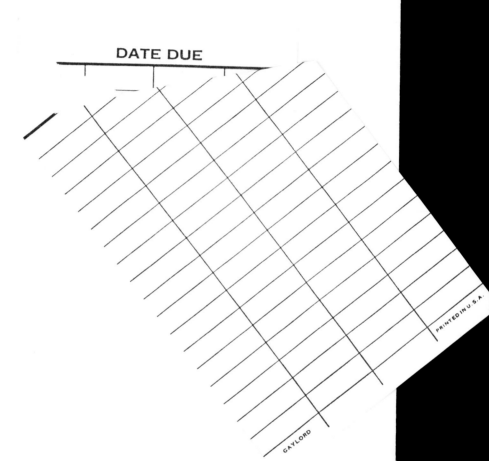

GAYLORD   PRINTED IN U.S.A.